Healing the Wounds
in Couple Relationships

Martin Rovers

Healing the Wounds
in Couple Relationships

NOVALIS

Cover design: Pascale Turmel
Cover painting: Private Collection, The Bridgeman Art Library
Layout: Christiane Lemire

Business Office:
Novalis
49 Front Street East, 2nd Floor
Toronto, Ontario, Canada
M5E 1B3

Phone: 1-800-387-7164
Fax: (514) 278-3030
E-mail: cservice@novalis-inc.com
www.novalis.ca

Library and Archives Canada Cataloguing in Publication

Rovers, Martin W.

Healing the wounds in couple relationships / Martin
Rovers.

Includes bibliographical references.
ISBN 2-89507-569-7

1. Couples–Psychology. 2. Man–woman relationships–
Psychological aspects. 3. Marital conflict. I. Title.

HQ801.R873 2005   158.2   C2005-900965-9

Printed in Canada.

We acknowledge the financial support of the Government of Canada through the Book Publishing Industry Development Program (BPIDP) for our publishing activities.

5 4 3 2 1   09 08 07 06 05

Contents

Acknowledgments 7

Introduction 9

Part I: The Dance of Wounds 15

1. Family of Origin: The Wounds Are Born 17

   Exercise: Family of Origin 39

2. My Wounds, As Best I Know Them 40

   Exercise: My Wounds, As Best I Know Them 55

3. Falling in Love Blinds Us to the Wounds 56

   Exercise: Falling in Love 71

4. The Honeymoon Is Over 72

   Exercise: The Honeymoon Is Over 83

5. The Dance of Wounds 84

   Exercise: The Dance of Wounds 97

Part II: The Dance of Re-creating Relationships 98

6. Re-creating the Relationship I: Know Thyself 100

   Exercise: Know Thyself 127

7 Re-creating the Relationship II: Communication 128

   Exercise 1: Communication 149

   Exercise 2: Communication 150

8. Re-creating the Relationship III: Emotional Connectedness 151

    Exercise: Emotional Connection 163

9. Re-creating the Relationship IV:
    Spirituality and Forgiveness 164

    Exercise 1: Spirituality 193

    Exercise 2: Forgiveness 194

Conclusion: A Family-of-Origin Story 195

Autobiography in Five Short Chapters 199

Glossary 201

Notes 204

References 209

Acknowledgments

Writing this book has made me keenly aware of family members and good friends who have made it all possible, and the coming together of these ideas, life experiences and clinical stories has reinforced that I am blessed indeed. This book is very much about what I have experienced in my family of origin, in my professional learning, and especially in my marriage, and it is with a very thankful heart that I see it now in print.

Many thanks go to so many people who helped me bring stories, quotes, theory and clinical practice together. I acknowledge those who helped me through the many edits of this book: my sisters Joan and Toni, my friends Terry and Maxine, Ben, Bernadette, Bob and Lorraine, Gerry, Linda, Colin, Theresa. A heartfelt appreciation goes to countless clients who have taught me more than I could ever learn from books or classes: those who shared their stories and their writings with me, and whose courage in facing life's "wounds" gave me the courage to put all this together for them.

Warm thanks to Novalis: to Commissioning Editor Kevin Burns, who believed in my story and accepted the book; to Anne Louise Mahoney, Managing Editor, for her professionalism and personal encouragement; to the designers and sales people.

This book is, in many ways, the story of my own family-of-origin experiences and how I was formed in the womb of my family. To Martin and Nellie (Dad and Mom, now deceased) I owe my life and the encouragement of my gifts; from them, also, the inheritance of my wounds and the opportunity to grow through these wounds; with them, the experience of family reconciliation and love. To my seven siblings, Joan, Ria, Arnold, Toni, Anthony, John and Nellie, with whom and often against whom I struggled to gain my own sense of individuation and intimacy, I give thanks for their unfailing love and support.

Most importantly, my deepest appreciation goes to my wife, Elizabeth, with whom falling in love, the dance of wounds, and the work of re-creating our relationship has been that real life experience that no book can ever prepare one for. Your love and challenge is the real story behind this book. To our daughter, Paulina, age five: I hope that a book such as this one might move you through life, love, wounds and healing a bit faster and wiser than I have done.

Introduction

This book is written for people who want to love and be loved, who want to know where love comes from, how it works, how love can live or die, and, especially, how to live a fuller loving life with their partner. Love is one of the most rewarding yet mystifying realities we live; in couple relationships, love has its beginnings in our family of origin. When we grow up, we experience love as it moves through the ecstasy of falling in love, wanders and weaves until the honeymoon stage is over, and spirals down to a low point in the dance of wounds. Love culminates in the awareness of how both partners are called to heal the wounds of their own family of origin and those of their partner and, together, to create a stronger couple relationship. A couple relationship has a pattern like a dance, with certain steps and rules built in.

Two people seeking to build a life together face a vast array of challenges and difficulties. Many people are frustrated in their relationships. Partners who love each other may not know how to handle the inevitable couple tensions and conflicts they encounter. Couples receive less and less support from families and society and seem further removed from sources of spiritual encouragement. There are few clear guidelines that can sustain couple relationships. This is all the more compelling because couple relationships today are based upon the feeling of falling in love or being in love. Romantic feelings are notoriously fickle and are often built on shaky ground. When love gets wounded, how does love get re-created? Long-term relationships need a deeper, firmer foundation, a clearer raison d'etre, and a better understanding of how these relationships begin and change and what ingredients are needed to make them last. Satisfying relationships with a partner are real and possible, but many couples need help to get there.

Fromm (1936), in his famous book *The Art of Loving*, writes that loving others is an art, and in learning the ability to love, we must proceed in mastering this art the same way we do with any other art, such as music or medicine. We need some mastery of the theory and some mastery of the practice. *Healing the Wounds in Couple Relationships* is about both the theory of couple development and the skills required to develop couple relationships. Together, they offer people the ability to understand themselves and their partner in deeper ways, and present numerous ways for them to re-create their relationship in a secure and loving manner.

When it comes to loving and being loved, we tend to react in patterns reflective of the past, specifically attachment patterns and ways of relating learned in our family of origin. These attachment patterns have become interwoven into our ways of thinking and being, thus providing an internal diagram or working model for being in close relationship with others. Over time, in a healthy relationship, parents' love integrates the child's inner experiences in ways that make it possible for the child to understand, nurture and care for herself or himself. This creates a space for the child's private personal growth and encourages him or her to move towards a more secure and mature attachment pattern. By contrast, in a family with immature attachment patterns, the child tends to function in reaction to others and is inclined to become either increasingly in need of others' approval or distant and cut off from other people. Attachment patterns that have been absorbed from family of origin can become interwoven into our present-day relationships with our partner and set the stage for the "dance of wounds" that all couples enact. Becoming aware of our attachment patterns will help us to know ourselves in greater depth. We then become better equipped to handle some of our own immature ways of responding. In this way we (and our partner) can become more acute observers of our attachment pattern. As well, this awareness helps us (and our partner) to focus on our own dance of wounds. Through this knowing of ourselves, we can bring thoughtfulness to bear in seeking new pathways towards a secure and mature position within the couple relationship.

Although this book is about how couple relationships develop, it is really about a whole lot more than couples. It is, first and foremost, about our family of origin, the womb where we developed physically, socially and emotionally – the primary place where our gifts and wounds were born, gathered and practised. As such, it is about the place and power of family of origin in our lives and how we deal with its legacy. We can let the wounds contaminate our lives, and especially our love relationships, or we can observe, change and enable our family-of-origin experiences to contribute to a new awareness and thoughtfulness of who we really are and how we want to be with our partner.

In brief, I suggest that each of us carries a wound or two, incurred when we were children in our family of origin, wounds that affect our present relationship with our partner. During the early stages of falling in love we were probably blind to these wounds. When the honeymoon stage gradually comes to an end, our eyes are opened, but some of our felt needs are still unfulfilled. The dance of wounds begins in earnest with our partner. Attempts to salvage the relationship by enmeshment or distance are counter-productive and the feeling of love lost hovers over our lives. This is the moment when most couples seek help, enter therapy or split up.

It is my goal to take you through the stages of systemic family and couple therapy, adding a good measure of attachment and emotionally focused theory with a savoury serving of why we choose the love partners that we do. It is my intention to be hopeful and to present a positive view of love and how it develops within us. For the most part, I believe that we have chosen the right partner, and we just need to get on with the conscious work of moving from falling in love to working on loving. Couple relationships are emotional and spiritual journeys. Love depends not so much on whether we have found the right partner, but rather on our willingness to know ourselves and communicate ourselves so that our partner may get to know us all over again, and vice versa. Exercises at the end of each chapter can help couples engage in renewing and strengthening their relationship.

This book is not a new theoretical framework for the understanding of love relationships. Indeed, I borrow richly from my own life and the experiences and insights of my clients in therapy. I owe a great intellectual debt to family-of-origin theorists, including Erich Fromm and Murray Bowen; to Sue Johnson and emotionally-focused therapy; to various authors, including Harriet Goldner Lerner and Harville Hendricks; and to certain poets, including Portia Nelson. I have brought together these ideas and experiences of love in a new and more complete manner, a sort of seamless narrative from birth, through love relationships, to the end of life.

This book is divided into two parts: "the dance of wounds" and "the dance of re-creating relationships." Part I begins with both the role and the power of the family of origin. Chapter 1 delineates how wounds can be born within our family of origin and describes different wounds that are often operative in couple relationships. Chapter 2 expands the development of wounds, what they look like and feel like, and how we can become more aware of our wounds. Chapter 3, which picks up the story where two people meet and fall in love, undertakes to describe what falling in love is and why we choose the partners that we do, especially from the point of view of choosing partners to satisfy unmet childhood needs. Chapter 4 exposes the sad tale of when love seems to be dying and the honeymoon stage is over. As our eyes are opened to the other realities of our partner, especially the faults and follies and wounds, we enter into a period of careful warfare and the negotiating of power within the relationship. Sometimes couples can do this successfully; often they can't. The challenge is to move from falling in love to working on loving. Chapter 5 examines the dance of wounds, the couple problems and the process and reasons for the fight that bring couples into therapy.

Part II deals with restoring couple relationships. Chapter 6 begins with the age-old proverb "Know thyself." The goal in this chapter is to change from "The problem with you is..." to "I have a problem," or more precisely, "This is my wound: help me." To know ourselves is an invitation to growth. Chapter 7 continues this theme, explaining the communication skills needed to heal family-of-origin wounds within a couple relationship. It is about how couples can talk to each other in significant ways to move through wounds towards re-creating their love relationship in a new and deeper way. The emotional connections needed for a good relationship to flourish, and the qualities and properties of emotional connectedness, are substantiated in Chapter 8. Chapter 9 looks at spirituality, which research has shown to have a strong correlation with happy couple relationships. Several aspects of spirituality are examined, including vulnerability, commitment and forgiveness. A seven-step process is outlined to lead partners through forgiveness to reconciliation.

Healing the Wounds in Couple Relationships presents an overall picture of interlocking pieces that make better sense when they are all put together. You may find that certain chapters speak to whatever stage you are in as a couple. In some ways, this is also a self-help book for people who are contemplating or seeking guidance for beginning a relationship – a first love or any new relationship. It does not replace the possible need for counselling or other types of professional help, but it can help partners understand more clearly the issues that could be dealt with in therapy. This book will also be very helpful for the marriage and family counsellor who wants to experience family systemic theory, especially family-of-origin theory, within the contexts of couple relationships.

PART I:
THE DANCE OF WOUNDS

I
Family of Origin: The Wounds Are Born

I walk down the street.
    There is a deep hole in the sidewalk.
I fall in.
I am lost ... I am helpless.
    It isn't my fault.
It takes forever to find a way out.
    —*Portia Nelson, "Autobiography in Five Short Chapters"*

The family of origin side is neither good nor bad,
it is just there with reactions, powers and dominions all their own.
    —*Carlyle Marney*

Family of Origin

When Elizabeth and I were married and the minister asked me, "Martin, do you take Elizabeth to be your wife?" the minister was not exactly asking the whole truth of that reality. In fact, it would have been a whole lot more accurate if the minister had asked, "Martin, do you take Elizabeth, and her relationship to her parents, and her brothers, as well as her other family-of-origin peculiarities, her gifts and her wounds, her customs and values, her mannerisms, her parenting style, her communication ways, her spirituality, etc.?" When I said "yes" to Elizabeth, and, when she said "yes" to me, each of us got a whole lot more than we ever bargained for: a partner and another family of origin, customs, values and all. Each partner gets all of the above and then some.

Interspersed with all the gifts and values we have inherited from our family of origin is a wound or two, perhaps in the form of an attachment injury or a piece of unfinished business. These family-of-origin wounds are born and firmly embedded in us by the time we are six to ten years old, a period sometimes called the "formative years." From that day forward, these wounds dance throughout our personal interactions. The wounds make their presence known especially in our love relationships with parents, with our partner, and later, with our children. They are like old habits, like "holes in the sidewalk" of our love relationships that we, all too often, fall into. Indeed, these wounds act as coach, director and choreographer of the dance we will present in our love relationships unless we make a serious effort to bring the wounds to awareness and inaugurate and master new, thoughtful steps of relating with others.

Like it or not, each of us has been given a family of origin, and this will be the only family of origin we will ever have. In a sense, therefore, family of origin is really just an accident of birth — parents and siblings we did not order or choose. So, we had better get used to our family of origin, try to get to know ourselves within our family of origin, even get to like our family. We need to make peace with our family of origin, because in doing so we are making peace with ourselves, with our partners, and with the world at large. We are making peace with our future.

Family of origin can be conceptualized as the living unit in which a person has his or her beginnings, physiologically, psychologically and emotionally. Accordingly, it is within the context of our family-of-origin experiences that our current self-image, values, behaviours, attitudes, and style of relating to and loving others germinated. To varying degrees throughout our lives, these early experiences can continue to influence our growth, love and development. We all have a family of origin. We learn to become social and loving people, or people with a wound or two, through our early experiences in our family. **The ability to love a future partner has its roots in how love was learned within our family of origin.**

I have come to appreciate the phenomenal power parents have to mould the lives of their children, for better and for worse. We can often recognize this in others first. We can see how some people repeat the patterns they have learned from their parents. A woman repeats the perfectionism about child-rearing that she hated in her growing-up days, while a man begins to drink just like his father did. A husband begins to withdraw from the marriage and becomes passive, like his father, while a wife becomes the screamer she always feared in her mother. Someone who usually blames others marries someone who often feels guilty. Yet it is more difficult to see some of these inherited interactional patterns and problems in ourselves. This chapter is about taking a hard look at our own family of origin so that we might discover why we act the way we do in our relationships. Understanding the why and gaining insight into the deeper dynamics of ourselves is the beginning of change for the better.

Harry and Sandra Chapin's song "Cat's in the Cradle" expresses this theme poetically. Children are born into families every day, and life is busy. Before we know it, babies become children who become teenagers; then they leave home, and older parents wonder where the time has gone. When we finally slow down and take time to look at life, we see just how much this child has grown up "just like me."

Many authors have written about the dynamics of the family system. Murray Bowen, one of the fathers of family systems theory, viewed people within the context of a larger multi-generational family system. He described families as a group of people with strong emotional ties, constituting an interlocking network of relationships; as such, the family is an emotional atmosphere that includes interpersonal relationship patterns, role-related behaviour and expectations, and the rules that characterize relationships. Family relational patterns result from combined overt and covert expectations and attributions of all family members. It is these relationship patterns and rules, strongly established within our psyche during childhood, that we live out and repeat with others, especially with our partner and children. Have you ever caught yourself doing or saying the very thing your parents used to do or say, even though you swore you would never do that? Have you ever, during a quarrel, observed that your partner is acting "just like his or her father/mother"? Most of us have. The fact is, each of us is, in varying ways, a whole lot like our parents. You can hate it, fight it and deny it all you want, or you can become a better observer of your own behaviours, see it happening within you and thoughtfully accept yourself for who you are, a chip off the old block. The good news is that, through awareness, we do have choices.

I remember the years in my mid-twenties when I more particularly disliked my parents. I felt that my father was a stubborn man who would argue that black is white before he would admit fault. My mother was a strong and determined woman, especially in the areas of faith and education. I disliked these qualities in them. Gradually, my siblings and friends started to point out that I, too, had a good measure of those qualities in my everyday interactions. I now realize that we often dislike those qualities in our parents, and perhaps others, that we dislike most in ourselves.

Family-of-origin theory understands the family system as a set of established interactions, rules, beliefs, stances in communication, and ways to resolve differences and conflict. These are learned in childhood and pretty much set in place for the rest of our lives, including adulthood. The focus of this theory is on the interaction among family members or between partners. Family systems change the way we look at relationships: we move from looking at ourselves as individuals to looking at ourselves as part of a larger family system. In family-of-origin theory, problems are seen not so much in terms of an individual person having issues or problems, but rather in terms of a couple or a family with problematic relationship patterns. Problems are reframed away from "it is your fault" to "we have a problem." Both partners will have to make changes to relieve the problem: both will have to learn to do some new steps in the couple dance to move it from the dance of wounds to the dance of re-creating the relationship into a mature and loving dance.

Maturity and Differentiation

Family-of-origin theory postulates that the degree of maturity we have achieved within our family of origin has a considerable bearing on all other interpersonal relationships, especially with our future intimate partner. **The key variable affecting the quality of intimate relationships with partners is the level of maturity or differentiation people achieved during the days of growing up within their family of origin.** In this book, "maturity" and "differentiation" have the same meaning. This ability to mature and differentiate gains prominence in adolescence, when the task of individual identity needs to be balanced with family loyalties and connectedness with others, such as friends and, ultimately, a partner. The mature and differentiated partner has learned to balance the interplay between individuality and togetherness, between individuation and intimacy. **Intimacy** is described as voluntary connectedness. It speaks of an appreciation of others and a closeness that brings out trust and reassurance. Intimacy, which denotes interdependence and connectedness and a place of emotional safety, is that capacity and willingness to want to love and to know our partner. Intimacy demonstrates signs of appreciation and closeness and involves deep, continuous and honest engagement and communication with our partner. **Individuation** is a lifelong process; it refers to the person's ability to operate in an autonomous manner without being impaired by significant others and without feeling overly responsible for them. The individuated person is one who is oriented by principles and can assume personal responsibility without too much fear or guilt. In short, individuation implies that we assume responsibility for our own thoughts, feelings and actions. It speaks about being able to choose our own dreams and goals and values and to plan to live them out. Individuation is that ability and aptitude that enables us to tell our partner who we are or what we want or do not want from the relationship. It is that courage to go first in communication or to reach out in acceptance or in forgiveness. The individuated partner is able to reveal themselves in the present relationship based upon a good sense of their family-of-origin past. These partners have taken a second look at their relationship with their parents and have arrived at a good integration of their childhood wounds.

Maturity or differentiation is that balancing of individuation and intimacy, and it permits a mature person to function individually and yet be emotionally involved with others, and to do both simultaneously at a profound depth. Mature intimacy is both an impulse for merger and a continued responsibility for self and a sense of autonomy. Couple relationships will always have that tension between closeness and autonomy; maturity permits us to be secure in relationships. People who are unable to differentiate themselves from others, particularly their parents, are likely to have problematic relationships with their partner. You can leave home, but you cannot leave behind family-of-origin patterns.

Bowen developed a scale of differentiation primarily as a theoretical framework to describe the varying levels of differentiation or maturity people achieve from their families of origin. Differentiation exists along a continuum ranging from poor differentiation to high levels of differentiation, with arbitrary numbers of 0 to 100 assigned to the scale.

A high score represents better differentiation and maturity where a person can be connected and intimate with family, partner and children while also being autonomous (self-determining). This person has attained maturity and security of self.

A lower score represents undifferentiation and immaturity in relationships. People tend to manage this immaturity in relationships in two ways: enmeshment and emotional cut-off. Both are very different – indeed, opposite – expressions of immaturity and extremes in relational patterns. Both indicate relationship wounds. **Enmeshment** is defined as ways that people give up their own self in order to please others. Enmeshed people have never resolved or untangled the original symbiotic relationship with their mother and/or father; they desperately seek togetherness by being loved, accepted or guided though life. **Emotional cut-off**, on the other hand, describes immature separation or distancing from important relationships, especially parents and partners. Cut-off can be enforced through physical distance and/or through various forms of withdrawal. Emotional cut-off can be described as the flip side of enmeshment. Relationship patterns vary because at one extreme, some people are distant from or in conflict with each other. At the other extreme, some people are too emotionally fused or stuck. Therefore, relationships can be viewed as operating on a continuum of enmeshment to differentiation/mature to cut-off.

Thus, Bowen's scale of differentiation can be reconceptualized like this:

Enmeshment	Differentiation/Mature	Cut-off
	Intimacy . . . . and . . . . Individuation	
0..........25............50 ....75 .... 100 .... 75 .... 50 .... 25 0		

On the positive side, maturity and differentiation have been described as the ability to balance intimacy and individuation, to balance connectedness and autonomy. Healthy differentiation or maturity can range between 50 on the enmeshed side to 50 on the cut-off side, a proper balance of intimacy and individuation. Bowen believed that no one scored a perfect 100. Thus, each of us will lean towards being a bit stronger either on the intimacy or individuation side of the scale of differentiation. If the family-of-origin experiences have been more hurtful or difficult, we can slant even further towards the wounds of enmeshment or cut-off.

The Development of Maturity

We are constantly forming our own identity. As we grow up, we are in the process of severing emotional dependence upon others, especially our family of origin. We move out and make friends. In this process of maturation, we are changing into a new, differentiated way of relating with our parents, partner and peers. How can we balance individuation and intimacy? How do we take a strong "I" position and, at the same time, maintain an intimate relationship with our family members and with our partner? One possible schema regarding the relationship between individuation and intimacy is that they form part of the same growing up and maturation journey.

The Journey Towards Maturity

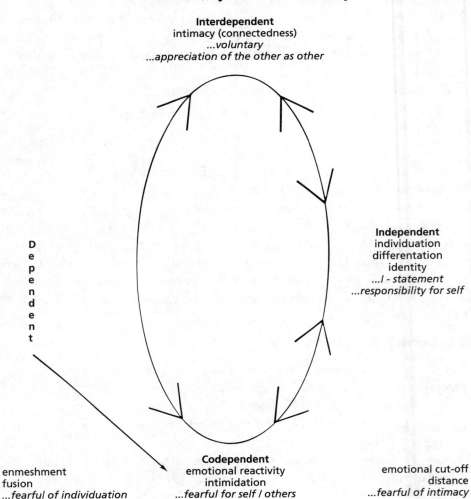

Interdependent
intimacy (connectedness)
...voluntary
...appreciation of the other as other

D
e
p
e
n
d
e
n
t

Independent
individuation
differentation
identity
...I - statement
...responsibility for self

enmeshment
fusion
...fearful of individuation

Codependent
emotional reactivity
intimidation
...fearful for self / others

emotional cut-off
distance
...fearful of intimacy

The road to full maturity moves from dependence to independence and then to interdependence. We are all born dependent upon our parents. We need to lean on them for many years as we grow up. Each individual's beginning is characterized by dependence upon another and, for some time, we continue to be dependent upon the family system in which we grew up. The development of independence happens gradually over the years as children, little by little, take steps towards independence by playing with other children, sleeping over with their friends, going to camp for a week, until they finally feel comfortable moving away from home. It is at about this same time that dating, love and connection with other significant people begins to happen.

Our journey to maturity can often be hampered by varying degrees of codependence when we remain stuck, to some degree, in the family-of-origin developmental processes of enmeshment (staying overly connected) or emotional cut-off (staying overly distant). **This codependence can also be characterized as different forms of fear. Enmeshment can be seen as a fear of individuation: a fear of standing up for ourselves or a fear of how others might react if we do stand up for ourselves. Cut-off can be seen as the fear of intimacy or connectedness.** As we get older, fear is reflected in learned relational patterns and carried into all our significant relationships.

Family-of-origin theory would describe this first phase of growing up as movement from dependence towards independence and individuation. The steps of individuation include the taking of a stronger "I" position in our family, and assuming responsibility for our own thoughts, feelings and actions. This may appear, at times, to be a sort of cut-off from others in the family. This can be especially true for teenagers and some young adults; cut-off and individuation are often confused. Simply described, individuation means standing up for yourself while cut-off means standing against others. It is believed, however, that the path from enmeshment to individuation might often involve achieving some distance between family members. We must leave the home psychologically, if not also physically. We need to achieve this individuation and space in order to become more responsible for ourselves.

For full maturity to be achieved, however, we need to move from independence to interdependence: the ability and desire to be connected and intimate with others, especially our family of origin, partner and children. Intimacy may, at first glance, resemble enmeshment, but the two are vastly different constructs. True intimacy has at its core free behaviour — a choice made by independent individuals to enter into a relationship voluntarily. Intimate relationships are characterized by interdependence — a mutuality of relationship that is freely exchanged. Enmeshment, on the other hand, is characterized by a largely involuntary codependence that seems to be threatened by the mere appearance of any degree of individuation. Because the enmeshed individual depends on the other for survival, any perceived attempt to develop an individuated self is seen as a threat to the survival of the enmeshed person.

Individuation may be a necessary antecedent to the achievement of intimacy as we move from independence to interdependence, bringing about greater ability to handle relationships. When we are able to initiate or receive relational closeness voluntarily, we have achieved intimacy or interdependence. Thus, the process of moving from dependence to independence (individuation) to interdependence (intimacy and connectedness) is called the journey towards maturity. On this journey, we need to examine if and how we have been affected by the codependent wounds of enmeshment and/or cut-off.

As the arrows on the journey to maturity indicate, however, this process of maturation can also go the other way. Some people prefer to move in the direction of interdependence first, and to feel secure in their connection with others, before proceeding to steps of individuation. Often both steps of independence and interdependence are happening at the same time. All routes towards adult maturity are fitting and, in the end, maturity is defined as the ability to balance independence and interdependence, to balance individuation and intimacy/connectedness.

Family-of-Origin Wounds

Two types of wounds can be born within this family-of-origin maturation process. Some individuals have significant tendencies towards enmeshment, while others have tendencies towards cut-off. Both are wounds stemming from the family of origin, and both demonstrate immature relationship stances. Indicators of these two wounds include the following:

Enmeshment Wounds	Cut-off Wounds
fear of individuating	fear of connecting and intimacy
too concerned about what others think	doesn't give a damn about what others think
scared to state an opinion	doesn't care about others' opinions
desire for strong closeness	demand for lots of separateness
"clinging vine"	"lone wolf"
gives in during an argument	"I am always right"
always needs others around	never says "I love you"
doesn't stand up for his/her rights	behaves like an irresponsible child
invasive	distant

Example: Mary and Joe's Story

Mary and Joe have come into therapy to deal with couple distance and continuous conflict, including verbal abuse towards each other. They have known each other for eleven years, have lived together for five years, and have been married for two years. They have no children. Presenting issues include family-of-origin interference, especially by Joe's mother, and arguing about affection and sex and about how much money can be spent on family members for birthdays.

Mary, the more verbal one, complains that Joe's mother controls him. Joe phones home almost every day, especially after a fight, to talk to and seek guidance from his mother. Mary has developed a strong antagonism towards Joe's parents, to the point that she will no longer visit his family. Joe complains that Mary is mean-spirited, argumentative and distant. His requests for affection are spurned.

Mary is the middle child of three, but functions as the family leader and arbitrator since her older brother is "out of it" from doing drugs as well as having spent time in jail. Mary has been in open conflict with her father since her teenage years and has "put him in his place." She does not care much what others think of her. She also has little time for her mother, whom she sees as weak and passive. Joe suggests that, on the outside, Mary is independent and capable; on the inside, she is depressed, closed, distant and cold.

Joe is the younger of two children. His older sister moved away from home to attend university and "rarely comes home." There is much conflict between the two siblings. Joe describes his father as his best friend and "my strength." His father is narrow-minded and harsh with his words. Joe describes his mother as kind and as someone who is never wrong. He feels her control, but renames it as concern for him. Joe relates how his mother can also give the "cold shoulder" when Joe does not do all that she asks of him.

Mary presents herself as distant and avoidant of her family, including a dismissive demeanour with her own parents as well as with Joe and his family. Conflict with her father in her early years set her up as the family "heavy" who had to defend her mother and other siblings. When family members turn to her for intervention, Mary tends to lecture them on what to do. Although Mary preaches a gospel of independence, especially for Joe, she presents as insecure in herself, somewhat depressed, and alone. Mary fought so many battles, especially for others, that she has not had time to really know herself. In therapy, Mary focused on her understanding of these family dynamics and gave herself permission to work on her own self-care and happiness. Mary began to see her own dismissive and cut-off attachment pattern and earnestly desired to reconnect "on her own terms" with others. As therapy progressed, Mary began moving closer to Joe and her own family of origin, especially her parents, redefining and clearly stating what she will allow and what she will no longer accept responsibility for. This more mature sense of connection and intimacy also enabled Mary to feel better about herself.

Joe presents a picture of a strongly enmeshed person who is unable to take an independent stance. This is especially evident in his inability to say "no" to his parents. Joe is preoccupied with what others, particularly his mother, may think and feel, as well as a strong need for the approval and affection of significant others. In therapy, Joe was ambivalent about early suggestions that he "leave father and mother and cling to his wife." He could practise this by phoning home less frequently and thus take a more independent stance from his mother. Even when Joe began to cut the umbilical cord, take some distance and assert a more objective stance, his comments exhibited considerable fear about the reactions of others and what his parents would think of him. As Joe began to individuate more from his mother, he found himself better able to listen to Mary.

Research has found that if individuation and intimacy are enhanced in our relationship with our parents, this will benefit not only the quality of our relationship with our partner and children, but also our psychological and physical well-being. There is a strong correlation between maturity in our relationship with our parents and maturity in our relationship with our partner and children. Another spin of this research demonstrates that as individuation increases, so does intimacy.

An Experience of Family-of-Origin Wounds

I want to lead you into an imaginative experience wherein you can recollect possible wounds from your family of origin. Recall an incident or a time in your relationship with one or both parents that was particularly difficult, strained or hurtful. Let it be an encounter that left a wound or limitation or problem on your interpersonal relationship ability. This memory might be from last week or last year, from your teenage years or your childhood. Relive this experience in your being. Picture the place of the incident; reproduce the scene. What happened? Who was there? Where did this incident take place? How did the actions unfold? Try to bring the experience back in full life and colour. Good! Now, add words to the encounter: What did your parent say? What did you say? Add feelings to the experience. What were you feeling as the scene rolled on? Were your feelings changing? How? What might your parent(s) have been feeling, as far as you can recall? What was the result of the experience? What memory are you left with? How does this experience live in you still? Can you notice times when this experience seems to "play it again" in your life? Gently bring the experience to a close.

Take pen and paper and write out the incident you just experienced as if you are writing a movie script or a play. For example, the dialogue might read like the following. In this experience, twelve-year-old William is alone in his room, reading a women's magazine he had taken from downstairs. His mother walks into his bedroom:

Mom: (with a surprised look on her face) What are you doing?
William: (looking shocked) Nothing, Mom.
Mom: (with a touch of anger) Don't tell me that!
William: (feeling guilty) I am reading this magazine.
Mom: (waving her finger) Don't be so foolish. Stop that now. That's not for you.
William: (pleading) But I just wanted to read it.
Mom takes the magazine and walks away, and William begins to cry on his bed.

Incidents like this happen often in our growing-up days. With the more significant incidents, some memory of it gets stored in the "pushed-aside" recesses or unconscious part of our being. This memory may be fleetingly awakened from remission and remembered from time to time as life's journey brings us close to similar incidents, time, words, tone, feelings, body language or persons. **The experience is real, and has left its mark. This is one of life's wounds.** Since our current self-image, values, behaviours, attitudes and relations with others are, in varying degrees, regulated by the experience of our family of origin, we are also regulated by these experiences of our wounds. I believe that we all have experiences like this in our memory bank of semi-awareness. These half-remembered experiences will become the wounds that we bring to our relationship with our partner.

Attachment Theory

Another way to look at relationships, especially as they were formed within our family of origin, is called attachment theory. Attachment theory has increased awareness of the importance of early attachment experiences on interpersonal relationships throughout life. John Bowlby, one author on attachment theory, described the process of the intergenerational transmission of attachment from parent to child. Attachment theory rests on a process that seeks to regulate our proximity-seeking and contact-maintaining attachment behaviours as children with one or a few specific individuals, usually our parents, who provide us with physical or psychological safety and security. Attachment behaviour is an innate motivating activity that promotes closeness and connection to our attachment figure. To feel secure and safe is the primary purpose for attachment behaviour. There are common variations, patterns or "working models" to explain the way attachment is learned. The internal working model is a representation based upon experiences of attachment from family-of-origin history in conjunction with current interactions between ourselves and significant others. For the secure attachment pattern, a delicate balance is sought between seeking proximity to the caregiver and exploration, between connectedness and autonomy. This is similar to Bowen's theory, where the concept of differentiation is characterized by the balance of two relationship needs: individuality and togetherness.

Attachment is an emotional bond that ties us to one or more significant others, especially parents, beginning in childhood and throughout our lives. Attachment has as its goal the achievement of a secure base from which we can interact with the world. At all ages, we exhibit our greatest happiness and well-being when we are confident that there are trusted people within our psychological proximity who can and will come to our aid should difficulties arise. These trusted and available attachment figures can be construed as providing a secure base from which we can go about and live our lives. The need for a safe haven in the form of an attachment figure is most evident and urgent during our early development years. A primary biological function of intimate emotional bonds is to provide such a secure base in and from which children — and, later, adults — can explore their ways of being attached with others, especially their intimate partner. Lifespan personality development involves the ongoing construction and reconstruction of these different ways of being attached, reflecting a dynamic and generative tension between familiarity and change. Therefore, healthy, functioning adults are not compulsively self-reliant and maximally autonomous. They are, instead, capable of trusting and relying on others, as well as providing a secure base for others, especially their partner and children. They have compassionate and loving relationships that are free of crippling possessiveness. The primary responsibility of lovers is to provide a safe, secure, emotionally supportive base that reflects the partner's current experience. (Chapter 8 will explore this topic further.)

Differences in individual attachment behaviour are grouped into three categories: secure, avoidant and preoccupied. Some people contend that adult romantic love can also be viewed as an attachment process, and that three major attachment styles are manifest in romantic love. The *secure partner* finds it is natural to become close with others and is secure in allowing others to become close to them. This partner, who is capable of both giving and receiving love, has learned to balance individuation and intimacy. Insecure attachment has two styles: avoidant and preoccupied. The *avoidant partner* is uncomfortable getting too close to others, even though they do want love relationships. Such partners may be less trusting of others because of childhood hurts; they are emotionally shell-shocked and fear getting hurt. This worry tends to hold back aspects of love with their partner; they suppress attachment needs or avoid distressing attachment engagement. Such a partner would communicate clearly that they prefer to have plenty of space and distance in their relationship, if they enter a relationship at all. They are the strong, independent type, the Lone Ranger of love who, from a distance, may look good in the saddle, but who will have emotional ants in their pants when their partner gets too close, talks too personally or asks too much of them. When this happens, it will quickly be time to "hit the trail" again. The *preoccupied partner* wants more intimacy with their partner — indeed, probably too much. This partner tends to suffocate and smother the other, feeling insecure when the other does not seem to love enough or as much as they expect or demand. They are so preoccupied with their need to have another person there for them that they fear individuating and moving on their own. These three basic responses of secure, avoidant and preoccupied usually develop into lifelong attachment habits with significant others.

Attachment Theory and Family-of-Origin Theory: A Synthesis

To illustrate attachment patterns, picture a wide range of normal development in the centre of the pathways, and abnormal development on both extremes. Using this multi-pathway schema, a full range of possible attachment patterns, based upon both attachment theory and family-of-origin theory, can be illustrated.

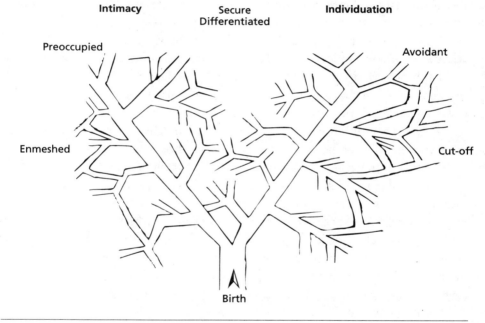

Pathways of Attachment Patterns

Enmeshed	Differentiated	Cut-off
0 .... 25 .... 50 .... 75 .... 100 .... 75 .... 50 .... 25 0		

Direction for Therapy

Towards further individuation   Towards further intimacy

33

There is no single route to normality or secure-enough attachment pattern. Development is not blocked by particular experiences of deficits, but rather rerouted or constrained into increasingly particular pathways over the wide range of normal to abnormal development. Even the normal or secure range is made up of numerous pathways, branches or clusters. The road to security is not an easy path, but a process that involves risks, choices and anxieties. Thus, early childhood experiences can provide a kind of relational map for managing current love relationships. These pathways visualize a continuous measure, moving away from set categorical traits. In addition, these pathways leave space for changes and healing as one experiences new attachment figures in adolescence and adulthood. Falling in love or the birth of a child can necessitate conscious re-evaluations of relationship patterns. Therapy, especially an integration of family-of-origin attachment patterns or emotionally focused couple therapy, can also fashion changes in present attachment patterns.

The three adult attachment patterns of secure, avoidant and preoccupied are presented in this schema along with Bowen's three relationships possibilities: differentiated, enmeshed and cut-off. Secure, differentiated and mature are given to have similar meanings. Directions for achieving greater maturity are also indicated. The Bowen scale of differentiation is included to allow graphic, albeit more theoretical, assessments that may help partners find a possible place to position themselves. Within this range of possible attachment patterns, and since no one scores a perfect secure/differentiated 100, there can be a variety of relational expressions that probably tip each individual's attachment pattern towards either greater togetherness/intimacy or individuation.

Pathways we take in life are dependent upon many past experiences, but especially our family-of-origin legacy. The central mature development range would be that secure relationship pattern consisting of an appropriate balance between individuation and intimacy. **On the one hand, there is a need for intimacy, closeness, affiliation and love. On the other hand, there is a desire for autonomy, freedom and individuation.** These apparently opposite needs, this dichotomy of desires, are part of life and may change in intensity depending upon the stage of life and experiences along the way. Some childhood experiences may have caused a person to incline or move further into the direction of enmeshed/preoccupied. Other experiences within the family of origin may have had the effect of swaying a person into the direction of cut-off/avoidant.

Example: Darren's Story

Darren came into therapy greatly distressed over his wife's statement that she wanted space from the marriage and time to reflect if she wanted to stay with him. Darren was in shock, distraught, crying and bewildered. How could she even think such a thing! He told stories of all the romantic things he does for her, succumbing to her every wish. He describes himself as a "romantic idiot." More and more, his stories revealed his strong need for attachment to his wife, to the point that he was smothering and clingy. Family-of-origin stories disclose that Darren was very enmeshed to his mother, insecure in activities in life and only left home at the age of 27 to marry. He recalls that he could never say "no" to his mother or his wife. In a very real sense, Darren has never learned to individuate, and his whole identity is tied up in being entangled with others, especially his wife.

Attachment Injuries/Wounds

My clinical experience leads me to conclude that all these family-of-origin and attachment patterns can be arranged into four clusters. Towards the centre, on either side of the secure/mature range would fall **secure/preoccupied** and **secure/avoidant** attachment styles. At the extremes of the insecure range would fall **preoccupied/enmeshed** and **avoidant/cut-off** attachment styles.

Four Attachment Clusters

Intimacy.................balancing................Individuation

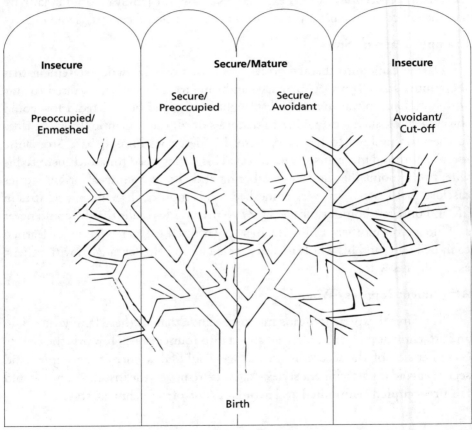

| Insecure | Secure/Mature | | Insecure |

Preoccupied/
Enmeshed

Secure/
Preoccupied

Secure/
Avoidant

Avoidant/
Cut-off

Birth

0...........25.............50............75.........100..........75...........50..........25............0

Direction for Greater Maturity

Towards further individuation ➤   ➤ Towards further intimacy

As a result of particular attachment styles developed in our family of origin, and since there is no one with a perfectly balanced attachment style, each of us will lean one way or another, either towards more togetherness or towards individuation. While we live and love within the secure range of attachment styles, we can manage the balance between togetherness and individuation, with a tendency to be a bit more either on the **secure/preoccupied** or **secure/avoidant** style. Attachment in the realm of these two secure relationship styles would be expressed in a more steady, secure and assured manner, and our wounds would be of less intensity than in the insecure range. In other words, these two attachment styles are within the secure range, with hints and habits of some wounds of either the preoccupied or avoidant side. Some wounds within the realm of these secure/mature relationships could be exhibited by a partner who does the following:

Secure/Preoccupied Wounds	Secure/Avoidant Wounds
• needs to know what others are doing	• shows less care about their partner
• needs to be given lots of information	• says too little about what they are thinking
• anxiously reaches to be assured	• fears vulnerability, inadequacy, weakness
• wants to take care of everything	• doesn't seem to care about how the money is spent
• has a compulsive need to fix things	• has a fear of failure, therefore I am not okay
• is quite bossy with the kids	• lets the kids get away with too much
• fears abandonment, unimportance	• fears being engulfed and lost
• seeks lots of affection	• is often not there when their partner needs them
• "I can't make it without you"	• "I need you, but not too close"

Expressions of attachment wounds when partners seem more in the insecure range would be more grave in terms of couple relationships. **Preoccupied/enmeshed** and **avoidant/cut-off** wounds would express themselves in more volatile and erratic attachment patterns. Couples can vacillate and fluctuate between enmeshment and cut-off in quick, knee-jerk reactions in accordance with felt experiences of being loved and appreciated, or not. Couples with these wounds do not have a solid sense of self, and they exhibit greater emotional reactivity. They deal with life issues on a purely feeling level and any sense of thoughtful response is lacking. Possible expressions of wounds in these insecure attachments range are exhibited by a partner who does the following:

Preoccupied/Enmeshed Wounds	Avoidant/Cut-off Wounds
• desperately seeks togetherness	• runs away if challenged
• is an emotional octopus	• is an emotional iceberg
• is too possessive	• is very distant
• gets sick when feeling unloved	• works late to stay away from home
• is a busy bee, involved in everything	• is a loner
• forever screams at partner for attention	• never asks how their partner is doing
• wants to be loved too much	• tends to love 'em and leave 'em
• "I am invisible"	• "I cannot be vulnerable"
• "I don't matter to you"	• fears others will harm or overwhelm them

Conclusion

Wounds are born within our family of origin and can take various forms of attachment styles, ranging from enmeshed to preoccupied to secure/mature to avoidant to cut-off. Each of us tends to lean on the side of either more individuation or more intimacy. Most people can manage their relationships with others in fairly mature ways; some people are deeply wounded and tend to be enmeshed or cut-off in their relationships. What we have learned within our family of origin, we will bring to all other relationships throughout our lives, especially our relationships with our partner and children. Becoming aware of our attachment style, and therefore our wounds, is the beginning of healing and re-creating more secure and mature relationship patterns.

Exercise: Family of Origin

This exercise is intended to begin a dialogue about how we see each other within our family of origin and the wounds that might still linger with us.

From what I know about myself and from what others tell me about my family of origin,

I feel good about...   I worry about...

1)

2)

3)

From what I know about you and your family of origin,
I feel good about...   I worry about...

1)

2)

3)

2

My Wounds, As Best I Know Them

I walk down the same street.
> There is a deep hole in the sidewalk.
> I pretend I don't see it.
> I fall in again.
I can't believe I am in the same place.
> But, it isn't my fault.
> It still takes a long time to get out.
>> —Portia Nelson, "Autobiography in Five Short Chapters,"

We are but earthen vessels.
> —2 Corinthians 4:7

We All Have a Wound or Two

We each have a wound or two because that is the nature of being human; it's life. It isn't our fault! There are no perfect parents. According to major psychological developmental theories, these wounds are developed within us by the time we are six to ten years old. Aspects of these wounds will be firm characteristics and enduring qualities. When each of us leave home, we pack these wounds along with our clothes. The wounds travel with us, even if we move thousands of miles away from home to "get away from" our dysfunctional family of origin. They constitute the unfinished business of the developmental stages, or unresolved issues of the road to interdependence, or skewed attachment patterns. These are the "holes in the sidewalk" of our relationships that we may fall into from time to time, out of habit. This period of relationship development stretches anywhere from age 15 to 25, and even to 45. For the most part, we do not see these wounds until we are older or immersed in a mid-life crisis. On this road to relationship development, there are no mistakes, only lessons, until we come to see and accept ourselves as we really are. A mature sense of self is in place when we can look in the mirror and accept and love ourselves as we are. These are our wounds, as best we know them at this stage.

Parents are human and, like the rest of us, they do the best they can, although some parents can fairly be described as more dysfunctional than others. Talking about the evolution of wounds from our family of origin is not at all about blaming our parents for what they did or did not do. Rather, it is about looking at the reality of our lives and naming it for what it is: a combination of grace and wound, strength and limitation. So for all the good things/gifts/talents/abilities that our family of origin gave to us, hallelujah! For the wound or two that we have inherited, let's get to work!

Carlyle Marney (1976) poetically expressed wounds in life in this way:

There is a shadow side at which I am always having to work: my wounds
What are these wounds.
These wounds come from old memories and distortions
and rebukes and slaps and no-no's and not-yet's and too much;
wounds might be oughts and shoulds and musts,
or you will or thou shall not
and the occasional gladness that comes unexpectedly.
These wounds are the 64 sets of genes alive in me!
Witnesses!
Forces!
All of them voices;
all of them parents!
In a sense,
this is the shadow side of each one of us
and I cannot bless any other side of me

until I can name and claim my origins.
This family of origin side is neither good nor bad:
it is just there with reactions, powers and dominions all its own.
For some, it is darker and danker then they would like to admit:
for others, it is an embarrassment;
for still others, part of my past that I need to accept and move on.
Wounds are given us by life,
by my situation, my culture, my religion, my sex, my race,
my economy, my class, even my climate.
They judge, they criticize, they influence me.
They are my mentors, my teachers, my examples, my powers, my ghosts.
Wounds are given to me with life.
I choose none of them!
I like very, very few of them!
I struggle and cope with most of them!
For what they have given me are largely scenarios of loss and shame and fear
    and guilt.
They pile up impossible expectations
and create no limits to my vulnerability.
I dance to their tune.
And in coping and not coping,
I likely made a vow and chose a script before I was even seven years old.
And I am still singing mom's song.
She knows it and I know it
and now my partner knows it too.
No one can bless any other
until he/she can bless his/her own origins.
I must be able to say both yes and no to my sources.
For the door to my redemption
is to be able to label my skeletons.

Wounds live in the gut, deeply ingrained. They seem to take on a life of their own. They dance to their own tune; when they are disturbed, they can lash out in a reactionary mode. It is almost automatic, something we do without thinking. It perhaps comes as close to instinct as we humans dare to admit. These are the habits that we are. Wounds are attachment injuries, the skewed ways we might tend to be with others or attach ourselves to others, especially our partner. Wounds can be words or tones or looks, and they remind us of family-of-origin hurtful memories. A wound is a break in the feeling of belonging. Wounds are like holes in the soul. Wounds are really about wants, which make them somewhat of a myth, for we tend to make lots of assumptions about what we want, or about what we assume our partner should know about what we want. Underneath the woundedness is a lot of I-want-to-be-loved-ness.

Wounds are not big, deep psychological problems that need psychiatrists to heal them. I am not talking about mental disorders here. Wounds can overtake us like a mood, a persona, a feeling, an automatic reaction. They are like old tapes, blueprints of our past, road maps that have guided us — nay, staggered and muddled us — to this moment. Wounds are our unmanageability. To change our blueprints is a very daring and creative act. **A wound can be described as the button that gets pushed, the trigger, the reaction, the gut feeling that catapults us back into an old feeling or pattern of action.** It is the "same damn thing" feeling, an automatic response, a knee-jerk reaction. Wounds are hidden in our character defects: some are concealed, others are just ignored, but they always catch up with us. Eventually, we are forced to unpack the suitcase and take another look, up close and personal, at the baggage we brought with us from home.

Intimidation is perhaps the greatest wound of them all. There are two main forms of intimidation: fear and guilt. We fear confronting the problem, and even when "the deep holes in our sidewalk" force us to take a good, honest look at where we are, intrapersonally and interpersonally, we can get stuck in fear or feel too guilty to face the source of the problem. This is especially the case if the source of our healing means an encounter or clearing-up conversation with

43

our parents. The feeling of void or emptiness can be the result of wounds. Wounds are often shrouded in the mists of time. Wounds feel like old times and all times.

Example: The Stuff of Drama

In the play *Death of a Salesman* (Arthur Miller), Willy is a 63-year-old man lost in the process of coming to grips with his own life and his failure as a salesman. He is tormented by his hopes and dreams, which have all fallen through. ("He had the wrong dreams. All, all wrong.") Willy wanted his elder son, Biff, to become the "successful" salesman he never was, and put lots of pressure on Biff to be successful in school, football and business. But Biff, too, is a failure at all this. The younger son, Hap (Happy), tries hard to please his mom and dad and constantly tells them lies about what he is going to be and do someday, but he is a dreamer, just like his father. ("My own apartment, a car, and plenty of women, and still, goddamit, I'm lonely.") Willy's wife, Linda, is the classic enmeshed enabler who continues to perpetuate the lie that Willy is a great salesman, and she forbids the boys to confront their father. In the end, it is Biff who is able to individuate the most within this family of origin, to face the truth about himself as a failure ("Pop, I'm a dime a dozen and so are you") and to challenge his family to admit to the illusion they have been living ("We never told the truth in this house for ten minutes"). He decides it is time to leave home and get on with what he wants to do with his life.

The journey to maturity is not an easy and carefree path, but a struggle for some form of differentiation from family of origin along with an ability to connect with an intimate partner.

Overt Wounds and Covert Wounds

We all have a wound or two. These wounds can be quite overt or seemingly covert or hidden. Overt wounds are those obvious behaviours that most other people can see and talk about: the lost son of a depressed father or the angry daughter of a distant, alcoholic mother; the inaccessible husband who is living out an early childhood wound of having been abused and forgotten and who can no longer touch his wife; a woman with low self-esteem who is still desperately seeking her father's approval. Some wounds have physical as well as psychological manifestations, such as depression, alcoholism and sexual addictions, but these are not the wounds. They are just the symptoms. The wounds are the hurts and pains that have taken root in our very being, compelling us to reach for that drink to mask or soothe the pain.

Example: Sammy's Story

Sammy recalls how, in his family of origin, he found the conflict between his mom and dad so loud and scary as a child, he would "sneak around the house" to find a safe spot where no one would disturb him or drag him into the fight. He would hide in his room for hours and pray that no one would call him. His habit of avoiding confrontation carried on into his marriage, especially when his wife would raise her voice.

We may not be able to recall a particular incident or defining moment that pinpoints the birth of a wound. Covert wounds might just be the atmosphere within our family, a lingering malice or a family habit. Wounds can be like shadows of our past; often we are still in the dark about the nature and reason for the wound. A wound of a thousand cuts is found in the person with poor self-esteem who was constantly told by a parent that his or her school marks "could have been better." Some wounds are less conspicuous and only come out to play in an intimate relationship with another person, especially in the intimacy of couple relationships. Some wounds are even disguised as good qualities, such as perfectionism, over-responsibility and caretaking.

Example: Justin's Story

Justin reports in therapy that his mother's e-mails often leave him frustrated because she "always" brings up some story about how his sister is doing "such nice things for her." This evokes an old sibling rivalry and feeling of inadequacy in Justin, who feels he has never been "good enough in Mom's eyes." Justin reports that he would then send off some sarcastic e-mail back to Mom, and the fight, the dance of wounds, would be on.

Unfinished business, in the form of unconscious childhood wounds or emotional reactions and buttons, may need emotional redemption within us and within our relationship with our partner. Such unfinished business can take many forms, for example, the unconscious need for dad's or mom's blessing, or the seeking of the same approval that we felt was lavishly given to one sibling and was withheld from us. Perhaps we want to hear three little words: "I am sorry." If we have always felt "left out," we may desperately seek a word or gesture of appreciation. Wounds can be present in the ways we love, communicate, touch, have sex, parent children or spend money. **Wounds are not our fault, for they were born in us when we were too young to be responsible. However, acting out of our wounds now, when we are in a love relationship, is our fault.** It is adult and mature for each of us to name, to claim and to heal our wounds so that we no longer trip over them, or at least trip over them less in our relationships with our partner and others.

Sibling Position Wounds

One particular place to look for the outset of wounds is birth order. A child's position in the sequence of sisters and brothers plays a significant role in future personality development, including wounds. Countless combinations of sibling positions, combined with other variables such as gender, genetics, space between siblings, stillbirths, events with parents, and even world events can instill particular characteristics in each of us, for better or for worse. All things being equal, however, there are some generalized strengths and weaknesses (i.e., wounds) for all sibling positions.

The strength of eldest children is their sense of responsibility, nurturing and achievement. At the same time, wounds can develop when a second child is born. The eldest, feeling displaced, may try too hard to be accepted, thereby becoming a perfectionist or a worrier. Parents are trying out their new parenting skills on firstborns, at times with difficult results. Youngest children are often special, and, as the baby, get lots of attention from parents and older siblings. Their giftedness can be a more social personality and cheerful disposition. Parents also tend to expect less of the youngest, in part due to the fact that they have experienced enough parenting to let things slide for the baby. On the other hand, youngest children often have less ambition. They tend to be the child in whom parents confide most, since they are usually the last to leave home. Middle children can be good mediators and negotiators due to their position between older and younger siblings. They also tend to be the more forgotten child, especially if they are of the same sex as their older or younger sibling.

Example: Siblings at a Crossroads

In the movie *Marion Bridge* (2002), three sisters reunite to care for their dying mother. Old sibling conflicts and family secrets rise to the surface. The eldest sister, Rose, has become the caretaker of the family, even as she stays in an unhealthy relationship with her partner and seems unwilling to really help her mom or address any past family issues, insisting that she is not "getting into that stuff again." The middle sister, Agnes, returns home after years away. She is also trying to confront her drinking and drug habit. With the help of her sponsor, Agnes has done some work to know herself better, and is now the family member with seemingly more differentiation and thoughtfulness and courage to look at the family issues. The youngest sister, Louise, has buried her life in watching TV and insists that "I have let go of that past stuff." As the story unfolds, Agnes is able to bring the family together to facilitate Mom's dying and confront Dad's incest.

Other parental and concurrent events also shape our personality, and thus lead to the birth of possible wounds. Parental divorce, illness, unemployment and frequent family moves can all leave scars on a developing child. A space of years between children can have its effect; for example, a space of more than four or five years creates another firstborn child for the one who comes next. I have a hypothesis that parents really do have favourite children. My experience in family-of-origin work leads me to believe that the stronger parent will tend

47

to connect more with the firstborn child, leaving the other parent to create a more special bond with the second child. This can leave wounds of family splits and triangulation, where parents may favour one child over another. Children are then forced into the task of being a "parentified" child. Perhaps the thirdborns end up lucky in that they are mostly left alone. At the same time, I believe that parents can love their children equally, but that this love will be different for each child: a particular look, a warmer snuggle, a harsher word. Many clients tell me that they know Mom and Dad loved another sibling more (or less). They feel hurt and do not believe it when parents try to assert that they love all their children the same, for their gut knows that it never did feel that way for them.

Sibling position is the luck of the draw. None of us has power over our sibling position; its effects can be long-lasting. Each sibling has their own perception and understanding of the family of origin, and siblings can look at the same family-of-origin experience, with the same two parents, and come away with very different feelings or wounds. Some children could end up more differentiated than their parents, a child or two might become more dysfunctional, while others would be left mostly the same as the parents.

Example: Fred's Story

Fred, age 41, was three years younger than his only sibling, Joe. His father was a church minister and the family all revolved around Dad and his work. Fred's father was a passive, non-violent preacher who laid onto his younger son the obligation of obedient responsibility. In time, Fred took upon himself the role and title of the dutiful son, while his older brother lived out the function of the prodigal and wayward boy, somewhat under the unspoken keep of Fred's mother. Fred came to therapy as his second marriage was breaking down. In both cases, it was his wife who was leaving him. As Fred recounted the stories of the marriages, he began to notice the common theme of meeting a women in need, falling in love quickly, and then gradually withdrawing and distancing in the marriage as his own needs were not being met. He said nothing of this need for appreciation to his partners. Fred's wound, born in his family of origin, was to dutifully accept whatever came to him — not to complain even as he became more and more sad and withdrawn in his intimate relationships.

A Simple Test for Wounds

When your buttons get pushed and the wounds come dancing, there is a simple test to determine whether you are acting out of your wounds at any particular time. Since wounds are unconscious in our youth and early adulthood years — indeed, they are primeval and reactionary in many ways — so, too, will our reaction be unconscious when wounds are kicked into gear by the actions or words of others, especially our partner. Therefore, as in the animal kingdom, where the natural autonomic nervous system response is fight or flight (or freeze), so it will be for us when we are faced with a "threatening" situation, such as confrontation or distance/isolation with our partner or family; we get mad or sad. Observe yourself or your partner for a while and note when one or the other gets annoyed, frustrated or angry — or, conversely, sad and withdrawn. Then reflect and see if you noticed and can express what happened or what was said just before the mad or sad reaction. An analysis of these words, tones and behaviours will offer clues to the buttons that were pushed and the wounds that were activated.

Example: Jim and Patricia's Story

Jim and Patricia have begun marital therapy. Both had very difficult, traumatic childhoods. Jim was the youngest boy, six years younger than his next sibling. As a result, he was left alone a lot, and withdrew into his own world. Patricia had two alcoholic parents and, as the eldest child, became the one who got in between Mom and Dad when they were fighting. As Jim and Patricia sat on the same couch, distant from each other, they constantly glanced over at each other, reacting to the other's body language. Patricia could get angry quickly when she observed Jim's habit of closing his eyes and turning away. When asked where she experienced similar body gestures, she reported that her father often would turn away from her and ignore her requests for attention or a hug. In the blink of an eye, she was thrown back in time. She felt insecure and mistrustful when Jim said he'd be there for her. Why did Jim close his eyes? When Patricia became too loud or argumentative, Jim was reminded of his father's anger, which he tried to shut out by avoidance. The dance of wounds was on: Patricia was pursuing his attention, and Jim was withdrawing in fear of her anger. Therapy was going nowhere as Patricia and Jim preferred to fight each other rather than listen to me. Finally I yelled, "STOP!" Gently I told them, "I know you each see the other as mean and purposefully doing things to hurt you, but in fact, you will only get out of this marital distress when you begin to see each other as wounded people." I reminded Patricia how brave she was as a child to have fought with her mom and dad to try to bring some peace and love into her family and her life, something she continues to do right now with Jim. I congratulated Jim on how much courage it must take to stay here in this conflict with Patricia when he was so used to running away by himself as a child. Gradually their eyes were opened to see each other as both a person with wounds and a person they loved.

Wounds are places and behaviours and feelings and opinions where we react with instinct, without thought or reason. We respond in an automatic, almost childlike manner according to old ways learned within our family of origin. We cling to the familiar old blueprints of what should be and an automatic reaction that dictates our way through life. When these expectations and needs are no longer being met, the wound explodes and our reaction is to be mad or sad.

There are other ways to determine your wounds. The test for wounds mentioned above, becoming mad or sad, is one indication that you have already tripped over a wound. With some objective hindsight, you might be able to determine what caused your reaction. Wounds can also be discovered by asking your partner, who is usually more than happy to tell you, what they perceive your problem or issue to be. Many partners keep a running tab! Another way is to phone home and talk to your father or mother. Because the wounds were born in your relationship with your parents, it is safe to conclude that the dynamic of the wound continues to exist, and one phone call, with the help of their voice, tone or familiar words, will bring back old memories and old feelings that will point you in the direction of the wound. Be prepared!

Owning My Wounds

We all are living the legacy of our family of origin: gifts and wounds. Yet it is not surprising that in the midst of all our good qualities and loving talents, one wound can keep coming back to trip us up and hold us back from our full potential to be, to love and to do what we really want. Wounds have that much power. The task of the mature adult is to be aware, acknowledge, come to see and own our wounds, and work on the process of healing them. We need to remove the power of wounds from unconscious, reactive and automatic places where they dwell within our gut, and bring them to a conscious, thoughtful and aware place in our thinking, feelings and actions. We need to name, claim and not blame our wounds. **Wounds are NOT our fault, but, as adults, it is now our task to do something about them.** Our wounds are always dancing before us. They are like lessons of life: either we become aware and take hold of them, or else we trip over them until we do deal with them and are healed. Beware: those who choose not to learn from their family-of-origin history are bound to repeat it. In that sense, our future is tainted in advance by the projections of our past. Wounds dance like an old partner: the same steps repeating over and over again, to the refrain of "Play it again, Sam." Wounds define our character, whose past goes before us like a beacon; we will keep going in that direction and call it our future.

Owning our wounds is not an easy task. Since the apple does not fall far from the tree, we are our mother and our father. Parts of their behaviour, attitudes and values are within us and we need to own this: to claim it, name it and not blame it on our parents. Rather, the onus is on us, as adults, to take care of ourselves now and heal our own wounds. It is our job now, our choice now, our responsibility now. The process of owning our wounds has been described as "an awful descent into myself." We can enter this process gently, mindfully, willingly, or we can wait to be pushed by our partner, or we can resist and remain in everlasting darkness and aloneness. Making the decision to do something conscious about our wounds changes everything.

Example: Sibling Appreciation

It was about eight years ago, shortly after our mother died, that all six siblings got together for a social evening. Only at this stage of our lives could we begin to tell each other how each of us was and was not like our mom or dad, and we accomplished this without too much denial or guilt. In fact, when I imagine the qualities and characteristics of my three brothers, lined up in a row, they offer a good picture of me, as I resemble a bit of each of them. It is who I am, and I have grown to accept that, and even appreciate it.

From Family of Origin to Family of Creation

Attachment theory provides the theoretical model to account for adult love relationships that concentrates on such issues as emotional bonds as well as adaptive needs for protection, security and connectedness with significant others. Recent literature has begun to examine the relationship between attachment patterns learned in childhood and adult attachment patterns in couple relationships. Important differences exist between parent–child and couple attachments, such as the more reciprocal nature of the couple and the role of sexuality.

The learned patterns of emotional expressiveness typically learned within the family of origin will affect every other relationship we have, both within and outside the family system, especially with our chosen partner. Therefore, it makes sense that when troubles come to a couple relationship, we can look in two places for a better understanding of the causes of these troubles, as well as for the solution: 1) within ourselves, in the here and now, and 2) within our relationship in our family of origin, where these troubles probably started as wounds. Not everyone is able to be in touch with or articulate the here-and-now experiences and feelings that are present in couple relationships. Some people don't know what they are feeling or why they act the way they do. Telling stories of what happened within their family of origin can feel easier, safer, somewhat removed. It provides a safer base and an experience upon which they can begin to comprehend their present reality and feelings, and offers partners a "why" to explain how the wounds are dancing in their present couple relationship. Family-of-origin therapy is not aimed at getting people to relive an old memory or to blame parents for all that may have gone wrong in their lives. Rather, a review of family-of-origin relationship patterns, from the "there and then," can provide a "working model" or blueprint of present functioning and thus help partners obtain a better grasp of the "here and now." Unfinished business of the past is probably one of the main issues partners trip over again and again in their present relationship. The old family-of-origin map/attachment patterns that we have followed for most of our lives needs adjustment and updating to better fit present adult relationships. Knowing where we have come from, in terms of attachment patterns, enables us to seek pathways towards the middle ground of a more secure/differentiated relationship with our partner. In other words, we can stand more solidly on the two feet of past and present attachment patterns by observing our family-of-origin functioning and by focusing on present emotional attachments.

Our family of origin is one of the most powerful, influential and formative influences in our lives. So much happened in our family of origin within our first six to ten years, we could say we are who our family of origin created us to be. Each of us has a natural curiosity to know our past, our family of origin. Most of us go through phases of hating or being disconnected from our parents, only to realize somewhere along the way that we really are a bit like each of our parents. This, too, is a step on the road to self-integration.

When we can stand on the two feet of knowing our family-of-origin past attachment patterns and wounds and our here-and-now emotional connectedness with our partner, we and our partner have two places to go to heal these wounds and re-create a new dance of intimacy. Partners are strongly encouraged to do couple therapy together so that they can address the issues that dance between them, for example, emotional security and trust, communication, knowing themselves better, and spirituality. Partners also heal their couple wounds when they re-create an improved relationship with their respective parents and begin to practise new attachment patterns with them. In other words, as Bowlby stated, partners have to adjust their working models, and since these working models were created in a person's relationship with their parents, it only makes sense to address the issues at their source.

Doing an extended family map (Chapter 6) so that we can know ourselves better, and talking over and communicating our wounds as well as our newly chosen attachment desires with parents (Chapter 7) helps us to unpack and sort through the many steps for which we need to take responsibility in our own dance of wounds. In other words, to change our attachment patterns with our parents is to change our attachment patterns with all others, especially our partner. This can be all the more essential if one partner is not yet open or willing to make changes in self or the relationship. Bowen strongly suggests that couple therapy can be done with only one partner present: when we change ourselves, others around us will also have to change, because we will no longer be engaging in that old dance of wounds that we learned in childhood and used to do in our couple relationship.

Exercise: My Wounds, As Best I Know Them

The purpose of this exercise is to try to become more aware and articulate about your particular wound(s) so that you feel comfortable to bring them into conversation with your partner. It is your responsibility to own them and share them.

One or two of my wounds, as I describe them now is/are ....

	Wound 1	Wound 2
The name I give this wound...		
The feeling of this wound...		
An image I have of this wound...		
I picture this wound being born when...		
The words of this wound are...		
This wound dances when you...		
One wound that I see might be operating in you is...		

I)

3
Falling in Love Blinds Us to the Wounds

I walk down the same street.
> There is a deep hole in the sidewalk.
> **I pretend that I don't see it.**
> I fall in again.
> —*Portia Nelson, "Autobiography in Five Short Chapters"*

Love to faults is always blind,
always to joy inclin'd
lawless, wing'd and unconfin'd
and breaks all chains from every mind.
> —*William Blake, "Poems from the Notebook, XXVII"*

The heart has its reasons, which reason knows nothing of...
> —*Blaise Pascal*

The Phenomenon of Falling in Love

When we leave our family of origin as young adults, we leave with both positive and negative characteristics, attributes and patterns of love imprinted in our hearts and innermost beings. Most of us then go on to seek a person to love and begin our own family of creation. In time, this will become our children's family of origin, and thus life goes on from generation to generation. We all seek to love and to be loved, to know another and to be known. The vast majority of us (even those who might not want to acknowledge it) fall in love at least once in our lifetime. When we are in love, we think we have found the most beautiful, intelligent and wonderful person in the world, despite what friends and relatives may say or think.

Leo Buscaglia, in his book *Loving Each Other: The Challenge of Human Relationships*, writes that loving, communicating and parenting are among the most important, yet most difficult tasks done by human beings — tasks for which we probably never took a course in high school or university. Because we have never studied these subjects, we do not really know ourselves and find it hard to connect with our souls.

According to Buscaglia, learning to live with and love others requires skills as delicate and studied as those of the surgeon, the master builder and the gourmet cook, none of whom would ever dream of practising their profession without first acquiring the necessary knowledge. Still, we fragile, ill-equipped humans plow ahead, forming friendships, marrying, raising families with few or no actual resources at hand to meet the overwhelming demands. It is no surprise, therefore, that relationships that often begin with joyous, wide-eyed naïveté too often end in disillusionment, bitterness and despair. Still, it rarely occurs to us to ask why, to research and analyze this threatening situation and find solutions that could guide us to more peaceful and lasting relationships (p. 19).

Several theories exist about the phenomenon of falling in love. In this chapter, we'll examine two such theories: 1) the bio-chemical view of love, here called the "cocktail of love" theory; and 2) the unconscious dance of wounds, here called the "needs satisfaction" theory.

Bio-chemistry: The Cocktail of Love

One way or another — by Cupid's arrow, a love potion sipped, a lightning bolt, candlelight, or the whims of the gods — we fall, literally and figuratively, in love. For some, it is love at first sight. Others take their time falling in love, preferring to develop a friendship first. For the most part, our Western society has come to think that marriage should be based on love, a romantic attraction between two people. In some cultures, falling in love happens as a result of arranged marriages. Falling in love can have as much to do with chemistry and arousal, proximity, needs satisfaction or good old true love. According to M. Scott Peck, in *The Road Less Traveled: A New Psychology of Love, Traditional Values and Spiritual Growth*, falling in love can be a sex-linked erotic experience, or the sudden collapse of an individual's ego boundaries, or "a trick that our genes pull on our otherwise perceptive minds to hoodwink or trap us into marriage" (p. 90). Put in a rather crass way, falling in love is life's way to suck us into procreation. Peck writes that falling in love is quite different from committed love:

> Falling in love is not a genuine form of love in that it is relatively effortless and it is not totally an act of the will or choice; it encourages the survival of the species but it is not directed toward its improvement or spiritual growth; it is close to love in that it is a reaching out for others and serves to initiate interpersonal bonds from which real love might begin; but a good deal more is required to develop a healthy, creative marriage, raise a healthy, spiritually growing child or contribute to the evolution of humanity. (p. 110)

This "cocktail of love" theory, which is gaining prominence, suggests that falling in love is like drinking a chemical, a cocktail of love triggered by social conditioning. It is the once-in-a-lifetime feeling that can happen to us a couple of times or more throughout our lives. Once we have looked into the eyes of our potential lover, chemicals such as dopamine, phenylethylamine and oxytocin take over. The dewy-eyed romantics are blinded to most other aspects of their lover, especially the wounds. Some believe that this chemistry lasts anywhere from six months to six years: long enough for people to meet, mate and produce a child. The intensity of the relationship and the tunnel vision of romantic infatuation give lovers the illusion of eternity, completeness, "the happiest day of our lives."

Consider, however, that if we can fall in love, we can also fall out of love. Peck states that, over time, the falling-in-love feeling begins to diminish and the real work of marriage needs to begin. He calls this the "discipline of love."

After the honeymoon stage, couples face the stark reality of either getting into the real work of love and relationship-building, or breaking up. Couples can decide that it is easy enough to be with each other and stay together. Love becomes a habit, especially if children are born into the relationship. After several years of being in love and partnership, you may also get to like your partner, and such a sentiment may be more important in the long run.

Alan Watts, in *Divine Madness,* writes that falling in love is

a thing that strikes like lightning and is, therefore, extremely analogous to the mystical vision...we do not really know how people obtain [these experiences], and there is not as yet a very clear rationale as to why it happens. If you should be so fortunate as to encounter either of these experiences, it seems to me to be a total denial of life to refuse it. (p. 23)

Many factors and situation variables can enhance or facilitate the falling-in-love process. These include the power of proximity, the role played by arousal, the traits of the beloved, and the role of beauty and character. Similarity seems to play a major role in a couple's initial attraction. My interviews with couples preparing for marriage reveal stories of similarity in family background, personality traits, ways of thinking, goals and interests, and leisure activities. Recent studies suggest that similarity seems to be an important factor that enhances attraction and helps facilitate the development of the couple relationship. It seems that more and more young people today are looking for someone who has similar attributes to their own. Couples may be following the "likes-attract" rule more than the "opposites-attract" thinking of the past.

We may subscribe to the "cocktail of love" theory of the power and purpose of falling in love, or we may not. I am sure that romantics and biologists would have varying opinions. The real point here is that, as nice and engaging as falling in love is, there needs to be something more for couple relationships to thrive and work. That something is called the work of loving and the work of relationship-building. We need to progress from falling in love to standing for love. Later chapters will expand on these areas.

The Dance of Wounds: Needs Satisfaction Theory

One contention of this book is that falling in love is a dance in which the wounds and needs of both partners, consciously and unconsciously, are attracted to and reach out for needs satisfaction and emotional complementarity. Love is a kind of psychosis one develops when there is space to fill in our lives. When we fall in love, we are reaching out to select a partner with particular qualities. We look for qualities that might soothe our unresolved childhood issues or wounds, and we seek fulfillment of these needs from our partner, probably at an unconscious level.

In her book *Intimate Partners*, Maggie Scarf suggests that both partners reach an unconscious "trade-off of projections" that have developed in each from unfinished business within their family of origin. In other words, partners "collude" with each other to reproduce old family-of-origin attachment patterns and problems in their present couple relationship. Thus, this may be, in fact, a certain fatal attraction. The characteristic responsible for the initial attraction with our partner (s/he is such a free spirit!) may turn out to be the characteristic that causes the most irritation and becomes the focus of couple conflict (s/he is totally unorganized and can't stick to anything!). The traits that initially attract partners to each other can become the core of couple difficulties once the honeymoon phase is over.

When two people are falling in love, and the wounds are dancing unconsciously between them, appearing as needs met and wounds soothed, what might this look like in reality? Here are some examples from my clinical work of the initial attraction that caused people to fall in love. After therapy and some soul-searching, partners discovered the pre-existing wound(s) that lay behind that attraction. It is easy to see the complementarity between the attraction and the prior wound.

Love Attraction	Pre-existent Wound
He was so gentle, attending to my every wish.	As a child he was never allowed to tell people what he was thinking or feeling.
She was so straightforward; I always knew what she was thinking.	In her teenage years, she was quite critical of her father and other people.
She was so exciting, and had travelled so many places.	Her family moved often and it was difficult for her to attach to anyone.
He seemed such a family man, close to his family.	He could not think for himself very much and was really a mama's boy.
He was so smart and analytical.	He was shy, preferring to spend his time on his own, a loner.
She could talk about stuff for hours.	As a child, she got attention by talking a lot.
She was organized and so capable.	She was an over-responsible child who had to take care of all the other kids.
He was fun to be around, and the life of the party.	He was given no responsibility as a child and got away with a lot.
He was so persistent when we dated.	He was scared to be left alone for a minute.

Psychodynamic theory suggests that we fall in love in order to fulfill or soothe or supplement our unfinished childhood business or wound. Freud's contention is that a woman falls in love with a man who reminds her of (i.e., is very similar to or very opposite from) her father, while a man falls in love with a woman who reminds him of his mother. Freud suggested that by the time we are five or six years old, having gone through various developmental stages to that point, our personality is formed and the rest of life is basically elaborating and repeating the lessons learned. This is especially true in the relationship patterns we learned from our significant parent; we seek to live out a similar relationship pattern in our love relationship.

According to Freud, the innumerable peculiarities in the erotic life of human beings, as well as the compulsive character of the process of falling in love itself, are quite unintelligible unless we refer back to childhood and see these characteristics as being residual effects of childhood (Freud, 1905).

In other words, at some depth of unconsciousness, we are aware of our childhood needs, be they attachment wounds or family-of-origin wounds. We search for a partner who, in the first glance and feelings of love, seems to be able to say to us that they can and will take care of and console that known or unknown pain we have been experiencing due to our childhood wound. According to this needs satisfaction theory, the most important woman in my life is my mother, with whom I had a 19-year relationship (before I left home) that was both affirming and incomplete, leaving certain love or satisfaction needs unmet. These were the most formative years of my life. Mom was a strong, determined woman who expected her children to achieve; my unmet need was to be affirmed, loved and believed for the good person I was. In my search for a marriage partner, these unmet needs were dancing in my unconscious eyes as I looked for that "one and only" who could satisfy me, whom I could love. How often have we heard the story of the woman who hated her alcoholic father so much that she went out and married a man who was the very same. Or the man who could never stand up to his overbearing mother and ended up marrying a domineering wife.

Harville Hendrix, in *Getting the Love You Want: A Guide for Couples*, writes that "marriage is…stirred by unconscious needs that have their roots in unresolved childhood issues" (p. 277). He suggests that we all have psychological injuries that happened somewhere during our growing-up days, at various stages of development. He believes that we remain stuck at the stage in which this injury happened, and that we tend to be attracted to and partner with people stuck in a similar developmental stage. As a result, we search for and select a partner with a certain range of personality traits. The traits that each of us are looking for in a partner will be those traits that "provide psychic satisfaction of specific emotional needs" (p. 279) – in other words, those unmet needs and wounds experienced in childhood. One of the goals of love relationships is to bring these wounds into consciousness, in order to bring about healing. Hendrix calls this work "the conscious marriage."

These authors emphasize that the childhood wounds or attachment injuries or unfinished business are not only connected to the reason we initially fall in love with someone. Aspects of this very same attribute or trait – or, better still, an opposite, positive, soothing expression of this childhood wound and need – are what continue to attract us to our lover today.

Example: Opposites Attract

A soft-spoken man who grew up in a family with a passive father and a controlling and vocal mother might be attracted to an open, vibrant and talkative woman. In the time of falling in love, the man may see the woman's attributes as a welcoming and soothing conversation, both because it is so much easier and smoother than his mother ever seemed to be, and because it comforts his own inability to make conversation. Some time later, when the honeymoon stage is over and the eyes (and ears) are opened to see the partner more fully and objectively, this man may begin to experience her conversation as loud, bossy chatter (not unlike his mother) and find himself silenced and withdrawn in the face of her power (not unlike his father). This will cause his childhood wounds to kick in. At first he may request, then demand, that she speak less and listen more. In a similar fashion, the woman might originally be drawn to his quiet, strong-silent-type ways. She may see him in a more favourable light than she saw her passive father. Later, she may come to realize that he is as passive-aggressive and hostile as her father was. And thus the dance of wounds begins for this couple.

If falling in love is a dance in which the wounds and needs of both partners, consciously and unconsciously, seek out, attract and reach out for needs satisfaction and emotional complementarity, then we must keep in mind and bring together three factors and conditions in order to understand how this attraction of wounds/needs satisfaction happens: 1) the collapse of ego boundaries, 2) the level of maturity/differentiation, and 3) choosing a partner of equal maturity and/or immaturity.

The Collapse of Ego Boundaries

Peck reminds us that falling in love has, as one of its stepping stones, the sudden collapse of our ego boundaries. As infants in the arms of our beloved mother and/or father, we probably had no ego boundaries or separatedness or identity of our own. We were symbiotically attached to our parent. Ego boundaries develop throughout childhood to adolescence and into young adulthood. As I pointed out in Chapter I, this process of maturation involves a gradual separation to the point of being able to stand on our own emotionally mature feet, what Bowen calls "differentiation of self." This usually happens somewhere between age 15 and 45. But it can be lonely as an individuated person, behind these ego boundaries, and we yearn to be united with others again, to be joined with one we love. Perhaps that is why we usually fall in love at about the same developmental stage where we are most separated or individuated from our parents. In other words, at this stage of our lives we are our most vulnerable self; our emotional needs and wounds and attachment injuries are fresh, unprotected and unfolded. Falling in love is a certain return to an infantile stage, a regression to the time of childhood when our wounds were being born within our family of origin. It is almost a babyish reaction; perhaps that is why so many lovers call each other "baby." Some of our childhood wounds, those attachment patterns that we developed during our growing-up years, are calling out for more contact, more connection, more affirmation, more "I-am-loved"-ness. Falling in love, with its sudden collapse of ego boundaries, enables partners to merge their whole person with that of their lover, be joined, and, once again, feel safe in the arms of a beloved.

Lovers, as lovers are keen to do, want to satisfy and be satisfied. We not only allow but almost encourage our partner to walk through our beings, our hearts, our minds and our souls as we lay all bare to them, including our wounds and our needs. We melt into each other. With one partner's wounds calling to the other's, two people decide early whether there is compatibility of wounds that tolerates the falling in love to go deeper. As popular songs put it, "I need you, baby!" Those of us with an enmeshed attachment pattern crave and love this experience, and, even those of us with a cut-off attachment pattern find warmth in another person's arms. Now the two shall be one and loneliness vanishes — at least temporarily.

Level of Maturity/Differentiation

Bowen developed the scale of differentiation as a theoretical measure of maturity. The scale ranges from 0 to 100 with the lower scores indicating poor maturity/differentiation in the insecure range, such as enmeshment and cut-off, while higher scores designate better differentiation and place people in the secure range. We each have a certain level of maturity/differentiation. These levels were described in greater detail in Chapter I.

Partners whose attachment styles lie in the immature/insecure range tend to have more difficulty with relationships. Enmeshment and cut-off are seen as prime indicators of emotional reactivity. (Emotional reactivity is the opposite of a good sense of maturity and differentiation.) When emotional reactivity is strong, people can shift from an enmeshed attachment pattern to a cut-off attachment pattern quickly or reactively, a sort of "need-you-desperately" or "dump-you-quickly" knee-jerk reaction. Enmeshed and cut-off people live in a feeling world and have difficulty differentiating between thoughtfulness and feelings. Enmeshed people are suggestible and quick to imitate others to gain acceptance or to seek out the ideal close relationship; at the other end of the continuum, cut-off people are avoidant or fearful of relationship, and are sometimes seen as lone rangers. Enmeshed and cut-off people are both in the realm of immature/insecure and these two attachment patterns are a kind of back door to each other. In cases of emotional reactivity, decisions are based on what feels right. Responses can range from automatic compliance to excessive oppositional behaviour. These people tend to meet partners who are the very same, or the very opposite of themselves, and they often vacillate between the two behaviours. Relationship patterns can vary from one extreme, where partners are very distant from or in conflict with each other, to the other extreme, where partners are emotionally fused or stuck. Partners with strong emotional reactions tend to choose people with similar or opposite reactions, and when the honeymoon is over and the conflicts begin, their responses can stagger between enmeshment and cut-off. Even when we choose a partner with the opposite wound, we are dealing with the same level of trait or attribute. Our partner is a representation of our wound.

Example: Paul and Joanne's Story

Paul and Joanne have been married for three years. Paul is the eldest boy in his family. His father was quiet and passive; his mother was strong and outspoken. Paul grew up and became much like his father: quiet and avoidant. He became a computer analyst who did not mind long hours alone at his work. Joanne is also the eldest. She seemed to choose her mother's talkative and enmeshing qualities. As the honeymoon stage came to an end, Joanne was asking for more interaction with Paul, at times to the point of angry demands for conversation and quality time. But it seemed that the more Joanne demanded, the more Paul closed down. Her needs unmet, Joanne would threaten separation. Paul would then try harder at times to be present, but never enough to meet and soothe Joanne's needs. They danced between enmeshment and cut-off. The dance of wounds was fully engaged at this stage and the couple decided to start therapy.

Secure/differentiated people tend to be more uniform and regular in their attachment patterns, treating partner and others in a similar and consistent manner. Even though one partner may demand more together time or some separate time, both partners have a better sense of self and seem able to negotiate the ebb and flow of each other's needs in a consistent and responsive way. Needs are being met in a more satisfactory manner, either by a better sense of self or by the responsiveness of their partner.

Equal Maturity and/or Immaturity

Bowen theorized that when we fall in love, we choose a partner who is at the same level of differentiation as we are. Differentiation here can best be described as emotional maturity and/or immaturity. Another way to word this is to say that we marry a partner of equal woundedness. Our partner is of equal maturity to us. When viewed through the pathways of attachment patterns in Chapter I, the wounds of both partners are of similar intensity, equal impairment, and equivalent distance from the secure/mature centre, whether this be on the side of enmeshed/secure or cut-off/secure. This can mean that we choose a partner who is either very much like us, or very much our opposite, in terms of attachment pattern. This would be the case if we fell in love quickly or if we were friends before dating. It would be the case if it was our first marriage or fifth live-in partner. In other words, this is an unconscious attraction of wounds that happens. Each person meets and "looks over" numerous possible partners, many of whom "do nothing for me." Then something "clicks," we fall in love and the rest is the history of this book.

If this is true, what about the theory that "opposites attract"? Research is showing that attitudinal similarity accounts for 81 per cent of the variance of interpersonal attraction. Is this reality or just a love myth to allow opposite partners to be seen as more compatible and attractive to each other? Perhaps we need to take a closer look at the word "opposite." It may have more to do with characteristics which, while opposing, are complementary. But how can couples be similar in some ways, such as background or values and interests, while also having an element of oppositeness and complementarity on other levels, such as needs and wounds?

Again, the attraction of similarities may have more to do with elements of psychological maturity, while the components of opposites may be more at the level of defence mechanisms. For example, a man who strongly needs to be liked by his peers might be attracted to a woman who is quite independent. A woman who tends to dramatize her emotions might be attracted to a man who suppresses his feelings.

The deciding factor that can help us differentiate those people who choose partners who are more similar to themselves from those who choose partners very different from themselves might lie in the level of maturity/differentiation.

People who relate in the secure/differentiated range of attachment styles tend to be more thoughtful and less reactive in their everyday affairs. People who relate to others more from an insecure attachment pattern, be that an enmeshed or cut-off attachment style, tend to be more emotionally reactive, and can wander and stray between enmeshment and cut-off readily and quickly. In other words, people who score higher on the scale of differentiation (say, in the 50–90 range) on either side of secure/differentiated would tend to be attracted to partners of equal maturity. People who score in the lower range of the scale of differentiation (say, in the 20–50 range) would be more reactive and very opposite to their partner.

From Dance of Wounds to Dance of Re-creation

Many people enter into marriage with very high, if unspoken, expectations: my partner will always be there for me; I will be loved unconditionally; I can say anything to my partner; our love will last forever. Gradually, we begin to see that we have not found Mr. or Ms. Right, or the ideal person. We are with a partner who has wonderful gifts and who also has a wound or two. Sooner or later, the honeymoon comes to an end, and at this point most couple relationships will hit the brick wall of disillusionment and pain, leading to conflict and fighting. At some stage, every marriage is doomed to some disappointment. In intimate relationships, partners hold each other in conflict as much as they hold each other in love and caring. Living in a love relationship brings both love and annoyance. When the honeymoon is over and the wounds become more active and needy again, we begin to communicate that need or want to our partner. Since our partner's wound is often complementary, or opposite, to ours, the couple wounds clash, demands grow in intensity, and the dance of wounds becomes full blown. Since the dance of wounds is really about the same trait or attribute, albeit at opposite ends of the continuum, the couple begins to create a core issue for themselves, a common complaint against each other, initially portrayed as disillusionment and conflict. These core couple issues need to be addressed in honest dialogue, or in therapy. Core couple issues where couples often encounter conflict include pursue/flee, over-responsible/under-responsible, demand/withdraw, emotional/appeasing. This conflict may be a shrewd, unconscious choice, because it is these core issues that bring couples to look at their relationship and perhaps seek ways to make changes. Because, in examining their relationship, each partner will have to review expectations, unfulfilled needs and wounds in themselves and their partner, we could say there is some salvation in our choice of a partner with complementary wounds.

Someone has said that there are two things that really move us and can create the energy for us to change: love and pain. People will go to great lengths for the sake of love and for the sake of the one they love. My experience as a therapist is that people come into therapy because there is now too much pain/hurt/distance in the relationships and one or both partners want to do something about that. Pain moves people to look at issues and possibly change. Hitting the bottom can be a great motivator. Whether we are moved by love or by pain, all of us will have to enter the real work of marriage and begin the dance of re-creating our relationship.

There can be confusion between the initial experience of "falling" in love and the longer-lasting stage of "being" in love – or, as some might say, "standing" in love. Love is not about losing oneself in the other but about standing and preserving our integrity, our individuality. Love is not a passive falling for but an active "standing with." The reasons why we fall in love will not necessarily be the reasons why we stay in love with our partner. Fromm writes that we learn the art of loving the same way we learn any other art: by understanding the theory and discovering the practice. Therefore, the work of loving must be a matter of fundamental concern: nothing else in the world is more important to us. Like the wall poster says, "Stand for something or you will fall for anything!"

Relationship Preparation

Since people are going to fall in love and since the dance of unmet needs will play some role in our choice of lovers, there is a couple preparation program that can enable us to take one good, long, hard and honest look at a potential partner before we sign on the dotted line of couple relationship and marriage. Since our wounds are born within our family of origin, and since there are usually existing attachment patterns as well as other unfinished business (values, ways of doing things, etc.) operating within our family of origin, I suggest that all lovers make a visit to their potential partner's family-of-origin home for a week, a sort of "getting-to-know-you" friendly visit. This needs to be done before you have fallen too much in love, while you can still be objective about what you observe. Enjoy your visit with your potential in-laws *and keep your eyes and ears wide open*. Become an honest observer and critical researcher of both your own and your potential partner's family dynamics. There will be lessons to learn in what you experience. How your boyfriend treats his mother or sister(s) will be an indication of what you might experience in years to come. How your girlfriend treats her father or brother(s) will likewise be signs of things to come. Observe the way communication is expressed or not expressed, how conflict is handled, what interaction patterns are at work, and the scope and expressions of intimacy and individuation. What is the nature and style of the family of origin's dance of wounds? What values are at play here: financial values, cleanliness values, parenting values, cultural values and spiritual values? What you see is what you are going to get, and a little bit less! The apple does not fall far from the tree, and a whole lot of the apples you see and hear within your partner's family of origin will be falling around you in your future years together. Upon that experience you can, therefore, make a better decision about continuing in this relationship or looking for a new partner with a different batch of strengths and wounds to share with you.

Exercise: Falling in Love

This exercise is meant to be both fun and complimentary to your partner, a sort of love letter describing what you like about each other. Each of you needs to hear what the other likes about you, so be honest.

What attracted me to you in the first place was...

1)

2)

3)

What I like best about you now (characteristics, personality traits, physical traits, etc.) is...

1)

2)

3)

What I like best about me is...

1)

2)

3)

4
The Honeymoon Is Over

I walk down the same street.
> There is a deep hole in the sidewalk.
> I see it there.
> I still fall in ... it's a habit ... but
> —*Portia Nelson, "Autobiography in Five Short Chapters"*

I've learned that no matter how hot and steamy the relationship is at
first,
the passion fades and there had better be something else to take its
place.
—*Author unknown*

"Falling out of Love"

If love is blind, then marriage is a real eye-opener! The honeymoon period of being in love, which can last anywhere from six months to six years, often seems like the time when partners feel most like they are dancing in perfect harmony, when they are in step, are open to talking and sharing and feel they are being heard by the other, when life is glowing. It is also during this "feeling in love" time when we are blinded to the full reality of who our partner really is. We expect our partner to love us and to soothe and heal our unmet childhood needs and wounds, but love cannot carry that weighted expectation forever. Our partner cannot answer all our needs. Our needs will also have to be met by our family, our friends, our God and a healthy respect for ourselves.

The reasons why we fall in love will not always remain the reasons why we stay in love. Gradually, ego boundaries and inhibitions that love may have laid flat between partners during the falling-in-love phase begin to spring up again. After the initial intensity, the love relationship takes a less intense form. We usually don't fall out of love; we generally stagger along in the dark until we reach the point where we open our eyes and see that our relationship has become different – maybe distant or even conflictual. For all intents and purposes, the "feeling in love" feels like it is gone. We begin to "see" that our partner has faults, habits that bug us, and ways that might even turn us off. Faults are exposed, disgusting habits are discovered, passion is subdued or even negated. Our Greek god(dess) is falling from his/her pedestal, and the realities of life are hitting us in the face again. We discover a whole new side of our partner that we did not see before, and we don't like it. Couple communication is one of the first places where these relationship differences or problems appear, and in a very real way, the fight for the relationship (for being appreciated, loved, understood, satisfied by our partner, just like it was in the beginning) is on. The dance of wounds has begun.

There are several reasons why the honeymoon ends and this work phase of the relationship begins. Falling out of love is often as natural and "easy" as falling in love, especially if our expectations of what love can or should bring are too high. Many couples in love are also fearful, and therefore hesitant, to put early conflicts on the table of discussion between them for the simple reason that it would be a sign that love is fading. Let us look at this a bit more closely.

Great Expectations

Gradually, any time between six months and six years, the feeling of being in love begins to fade and the honeymoon draws to a close. Old wounds begin to show their ugly face – or, put more accurately, old family-of-origin patterns of relating, loving and communicating reassert themselves. We see our partner's faults in a new way, if not for the first time. Love might be blind, but in time, being in a couple relationship opens our eyes to the whole person. If marriage is for better or worse, the worse is now coming forward – gradually, but surely. People often say that their partner has changed and that this is not the man or woman they fell in love with. Indeed, although it may feel like the other has changed, in fact, most often the other partner has simply gone back to old ways of doing things, and old family-of-origin wounds are presenting themselves. Old family-of-origin winds can blow pretty strong. These wounds were there all along, although perhaps covered over while the couple was in love as each partner put their best foot forward.

Every marriage is doomed to some disillusionment. "And they lived happily ever after" is one of the most tragic sentences in literature, because it speaks a certain falsehood about life and love and sets up expectations that are not at all possible for frail human beings. Since people are most charming during the dating time, partners are frequently misled in the sense that they do not fully know their partner yet. Each person, I believe, hides some stuff in that deep, dark corner of their soul. So when the experiences of disillusionment come, it may feel like our partner is mean or inadequate or incompetent because they seem to stop giving us what we need and our relationship feels like it is failing. Falling out of love does not mean that we stop loving, but it is a crisis time when the nature and expressions of love need to change.

A large part of the problem is due to unrealistic expectations for the relationship. Our society has learned to set up such high standards that few can ever meet them. In particular, people expect to get all of their emotional needs met within this one relationship, which is completely unrealistic. When people begin to feel cheated by their partner's seeming lack of love, they begin to make demands of their partner to change, what Virginia Satir calls the Big Game of Life. In this game, people assume they have a right to expect satisfaction of their emotional needs from their partner, and some partners begin to push for these changes in the relationship. Partners talk and act like it is only the other person who has to change. Such intolerance in a relationship creates distance between the partners.

In our sadness, hurt and desperation, our first impulse is to blame the other for changing, for whatever reason: for cruelly, purposely, meanly withdrawing their love and causing all this pain. Why have you changed? we ask. Worse yet, you have changed so much that now you even look and act like my father/mother did when he/she was so mean. What we want is to be able to go back to the way it was, when we experienced those blissful feelings of being in love not so long ago. In family systems psychology, we call this homeostasis — the desire to return to the old and familiar — a powerful force in couples and families. We have been doing it this way for the past so many years; why do you want to change it now? Families often do not allow or encourage people to change or to rock the boat. Families want to hold people in their place. It was safe and comfortably secure then; let's go back to the days when love was blind. But there is no going back; there is only going ahead, and perhaps through this crisis called falling out of love, we move towards a new, deeper loving.

And so the dance of wounds begins. The fight will be to get our partner back to where s/he was when all was well and love was strong: the fight is to feel those feelings of being in love again, when we were cared for, desired, appreciated, understood; the fight for love when we dared to say it all, think it all, feel it all and do it all; the fight for communication that used to hold us and keep us in such good stead and maintained that feeling of being in love; the fight for survival; the fight for the dream that is changing and getting lost right before our eyes.

The dance of love is ending and the dance of wounds has begun. Communication begins to spiral in a negative direction, and word leads to heated word, tone brings on angry tone, and look provokes hurtful look. Both blame the other. Rarely does either see their own contribution to the problem, and soon repetitive, negative communication patterns develop. It is not that we fall out of love overnight; it is more like two steps forward and one step back. Couples can have a small quarrel and make up; then this becomes a bigger conflict and another making up. Finally, it becomes an ongoing fight because we are not getting what we want and need from our partner. Many couples seem to need ten fights over any particular issue to learn not to fight in that way anymore, or to seek another way to handle the issue. Who will break this destructive cycle of interaction and communication? Who is big enough to go first and seek a different frame on the couple problem? Can the dance of wounds be stopped? Falling out of love does not mean we stop loving. How can we move from falling in love to working on loving, for the nature and expression of love needs to change?

Example: Falling in Love Again

A man who was giving a marriage enrichment talk with his wife told us that around his eighth year of marriage, he woke up one morning, looked at his wife lying next to him in bed and thought to himself, "I just don't love her." He related how he decided to court her again, taking her out to dinner, etc. He said that six months later he was in love again. He was doing the work of re-creating a relationship, but all partners are not so wise.

Falling out of Love

Couples come to therapy complaining about their relationship and/or sex life, and how it has evolved from when they were first in love. The spark has gone out of their love, in part perhaps because of busy lives, children and various life events. Too many people hold on to the fallacy of romantic love as gospel truth. The euphoria of initial love was never meant to last a lifetime, as we saw in the last chapter. Love seeks and requires other expressions that are as meaningful and warm as romantic love. Falling in love needs to change to the work of loving. Couple distance begins to set in, and some warning signs are recognizable. I want to explore these warning signs on two levels: on the level of couple behaviours and on the deeper level of the dance of wounds.

On the level of observable behaviours, one of the first red flags in the loss of initial love in a couple relationship is the change from loving communication to complaints, nagging, frustration and criticism. Communication time becomes shorter, often more tense and judgmental, and most signs of affirmation, appreciation and caring are lost. This is followed by a decline in affection, for when unresolved disappointment and frustration increases, affection decreases. It is hard to hug someone who has just criticized you. A stalemate develops as both partners try harder to get the other back to the loving ways of before, only to meet with rejection or failure. Couples begin to wall themselves off from each other; attempts to initiate love decrease; no one makes a first move. Often couples complain bitterly about how mean their partner is to be doing this, and question why they would withhold love on purpose. The last warning sign is couple distance, where one partner spends more and more time away, or where one partner becomes depressed or overly critical and angry. The dance of wounds is in full force!

Example: A Broken Record

Wife to husband: "If I told you once, I have told you a thousand times..."
Therapist to wife: "Stop! Really a thousand times?
Wife to therapist: "At least!"
Therapist to wife: "Then what makes you think that a thousand and one times will make him hear you or change anything now?"

Frequency and volume do not help when people are stuck in the dance of wounds. Trying harder will be of no avail, other than to maintain a stuck way of interacting between partners. Partners will need to address this impasse from some other direction and enter through some other door. Someone must stop the merry-go-round this couple is on and become thoughtful about doing something differently.

On the level of the deeper dance of wounds, several warning signs can help partners clue in that all is not well in the couple relationship. These warning signs will come from the deeper gut, so they are less obvious, but they can be detected with careful hindsight. The first warning sign is the simple test for wounds presented in Chapter 2: namely, when one person has a sudden rush of intense emotions, such as anger or sadness. When this happens, your reaction tends to be one of self-defence, by either withdrawing or acting aggressively. The unconscious wounds are ringing loud bells to let you know that something is wrong and you do not like it. A second warning sign is the experience of an old and familiar feeling, which, if you reflect and stay with it, will probably bring you back to some childhood experience. It might be an old feeling of guilt when your partner requests or demands something or is critical, a feeling that you first experienced with a significant parent. In other words, experiences with partners can be passed through old perceptions and assumptions we have grown used to. Other old wound feelings can be frustration, anxiety or resentment. When we are in touch with this old feeling, we almost want to ask if it is our partner or our parent in the room right now. There is a recurring aspect to this old feeling, especially when the intensity of the feeling is out of proportion to our partner's actions or words. The most powerful feeling of an old wound kicking in is the feeling of rejection and/or insecurity. The dance of wounds can also have a conflictual side, which can bring partners back to childhood feelings of abuse or rejection. This is a sign that the relationship is no longer safe.

Wounds are places and behaviours and feelings and opinions where we react or respond in an assumed, automatic, almost childlike manner according to old ways learned within our family of origin. We cling to the familiar, to old blueprints of what should be, and we exhibit an automatic reaction that dictates our way through life. When these expectations and needs are no longer being met, the wound kicks in and we react by feeling mad or sad, with distance or with attempts to enmesh.

Example: Hidden Feelings

A woman who does not like the way her partner makes decisions unilaterally might shy away from saying anything for fear of rocking the boat and for fear that he might leave. A man annoyed by his partner's chat about girlfriends and shopping just smiles. He doesn't want to rock the boat either.

It is these fears and growing dissatisfactions with our partner that usher in this stage of the honeymoon's end. When ignored too long, they can turn into anger, disappointment or passive aggression. In other words, needs and wants are beginning to be unfulfilled. There is a growing sense of insecurity in our relationship with our partner. One partner may begin to distance more, or become more preoccupied with the relationship. This, in fact, is what launches the process of the dance of wounds.

The Unconscious Matching of Wounds

The unconscious matching of wounds can be damaging to the ensuing relationship of love. We each have a wound or two, and since partners are matched by unconscious forces or by random choice, sooner or later these wounds will show themselves in the couple relationship. Wounds are really about wants and unmet needs, and so they are somewhat of a myth, for we tend to make a lot of assumptions about what we want, or about what we assume our partner should know about what we want. These are the love knots or binds that many couples can get themselves into during this falling-out-of-love stage. Gordon (1990) describes love knots as assumptions partners make, often unspoken, about what love is or should be for them; they look to their partner for fulfillment of these expectations and assumptions. But because so many of these are unspoken and therefore unknown by the other partner, they become dangerous assumptions that can leave both partners looking foolish. Here are a few examples:

1) If you really loved me, you would give me what I need. Since you do not give me what I need, you obviously do not love me, and so I will withhold my love from you.

2) Weekends are family time. If you have any desire to be part of our family, you would want to stay home and do things with us.

3) If you really wanted to listen to me, you would look at me and say nothing until I am finished. So why are you looking away from me?

Different with Family and Friends

Have you ever noticed that we seem to react differently to partners and parents than we do to co-workers and friends? It seems that family, partners and children bring out emotional reactions that are more primeval, gut, automatic, visceral, from the heart. Many people have observed that they are capable of both communicating with and confronting friends and co-workers, but tell stories of "losing it" when they come home to their partners or parents or children. Apparently, a whole different dynamic, which Bowen called "emotional reactivity," is at play here. These emotional reactions can be moulded over generations, but are learned within our family of origin: that is why we are more reactive in relationship to parents, partners and children. Our emotional reactions to them seem to come from the gut level, with deep-down emotions – the in-wounds – while dealing with co-workers can be more distant and objective – the out-wounds. These two realms can get blurred when our boss at work just happens to remind us a whole lot of our mother or father.

Decision Time

Love is a temporary madness; it erupts like volcanoes and then it subsides. And when it subsides, you have to make a decision. You have to work out whether your roots have entwined together that it is inconceivable that you should ever part. Because this is what love is ... love itself is what is left over when being in love has burned away, and this is both an art and a fortunate accident. (Louis de Bernières [1994], *Captain Corelli's Mandolin*)

After the falling in love, after the honeymoon is over, and after the reciprocal fighting has been going on for some time, we must decide either to begin the work of re-creating the couple relationship, to muddle on for some more years, or to terminate the relationship. If, as a couple, you have stagnated for some time, it is time to do something different. Staying in the negative, downward spiral only means a repetition of the same old thing, perhaps with a different tone of anger or a different level of depression. Give yourselves this little test: if you have danced the same dance of wounds five to ten times in the past year, if you have noticed that you end up in that same hole in the sidewalk, or tried very hard and gone nowhere, it is time for something completely different. Turning to a good friend, a mentor, a good book or a good therapist can be an excellent starting point.

Coming to Counselling

Even though falling out of love is a difficult and taxing time, it can be the beginning of a new phase in your relationship. It may feel like a crisis but it has, hidden within its fire, the possibilities of new opportunity, a need to get to know your partner in new and deeper ways. In a sense, the honeymoon has to end so new things can begin. Too often couples wait too long before coming to counselling. They think therapy is for those whose relationship is "really bad," or even for those who are downright crazy, and they wait until things have gone too far.

I prefer to work with couples before they get married, or within the first few years of the relationship. Change and growth and healing are possible with couples who trust and love each other and want to change and grow. Coming early to counselling is the best guarantee of success. My experience as a therapist tells me that when couples come early enough, most relationships can be revamped and revitalized, but if there is too much dirty water under the bridge, and if the love has been damaged too much, it is difficult for couples to regain the trust and desire they need to re-create the relationship.

We heard earlier that the three greatest things we human beings do in life — to love, to communicate and to parent — are not taught in school or university, and yet we all think we are experts on these subjects. The fact is that we are experts on these matters to much the same degree and in the same fashion as we learned them in our families of origin, often tripping over the same mistakes and wounds. To become aware of ourselves, and to thoughtfully see other ways of loving, communicating and parenting requires new learning. Just as we must get regular check-ups from our doctor to maintain healthy bodies, we must have a relationship check-up periodically. A weekend away, or several sessions with a therapist to talk through the conflictual issues in their genesis, can smooth the road for the future.

A TV commercial years ago for the Fram oil filter showed a man and an auto mechanic standing in front of the man's car. The hood is up and smoke is pouring from the blown motor. A repaired or new motor could cost a thousand dollars. The mechanic is holding a $3.95 Fram oil filter and telling the man that he should have been buying these for his car all along, for "you can pay me now [for an oil filter] or you can pay me later [for a new motor]." If the car represents a relationship, the oil filters represent sessions with a therapist. Therapists are much cheaper than lawyers, and the results are much more rewarding.

Exercise: The Honeymoon Is Over

This is a "get honest" exercise for you as a couple to help you begin to become aware of the early steps in your dance of wounds. This exercise is not about blame but observation of what both of you see as unhelpful or hurting patterns in your relationship.

The things you do that bug me, that get me mad or sad, are

1)

2)

3)

We seem to fight over these issues again and again...

1)

2)

3)

We often end up in this same spot where...

5
The Dance of Wounds

I walk down the same street.
> There is a deep hole in the sidewalk.
> I pretend I don't see it.
> I fall in again.
I can't believe I am in the same place.
> > But, it isn't my fault.
It still takes a long time to get out.
—*Portia Nelson, "Autobiography in Five Short Chapters"*

The dance of wounds
> is the dance of all persons.
It will continue a dance of wounds and hurting
> until such time,
> > through awareness and thoughtfulness
that I change it into
> a dance of life and self-understanding
> > that can even lead to
> > > a dance of joy.
—*Martin Rovers*

Conjugal soul-making is choreographic.
—*Kohlbenschlag*

The Dance Begins

All of us want to be loved. Falling in love offers both partners the feeling and assurance that some fundamental unmet needs are being appeased, such as intimacy, affiliation, individuation, achievement, and so on. When the honeymoon begins to wane, however, and one partner begins to get the impression that these primary needs are being ignored too much by the other partner, this situation can create what is called "primary distress." In response to this perceived lack of attention or distance in attachment patterns, partners seek, often desperately, a return to that previous "falling in love" feeling. But as we have seen, that sort of love intensity cannot be maintained, the honeymoon comes to an end, and the dance of wounds begins.

In Chapter I, family-of-origin theory described the family system as a set of established interactions, rules, beliefs, stances in communication, and ways to resolve differences and conflict. These are learned in childhood within our family of origin and are pretty much set in place and operative for the rest of our lives. The focus is on the interactions that occur among family members or between partners. Systemic theory suggests that these interactions tend to be reciprocal, patterned, spiral and repetitive. When these interactions are on the hurting or fighting side, the dance of wounds begins to take over. These dance steps of hurt and anger are reciprocal: one event modifies another which in turn modifies the first. **The "dance" between family members or between partners happens when the behaviour, words, tone or look of one person dovetails with or causes an emotional reaction in the other.** Each couple will, by trial and error, determine their own unique dance of wounds. This dance is reciprocal in that it is never possible to find out who really started it, although couples at the beginning of therapy are most willing to point fingers and shout that it is "all your fault!" This dance is also patterned and repetitive: the "same old thing" happens often enough that couples in therapy can tell stories, or as one wife put it, "If I've told you once, I've told you a thousand times!" Spiral refers to this dance progressing from bad to worse (negative spiral) and creating distance in the couple relationship, or advancing gradually to a better situation (positive spiral), which can help bring partners together.

This dance of wounds, these circular loops of hurt and anger, acquire their beginnings within our family of origin and are continued with more or less repetition within our intimate couple relationship. The steps of this dance are so well rehearsed that both partners know them instinctively, although perhaps not consciously. Thus the overfunctioning partner (the one who takes the lead and takes charge of couple business) shapes the attitudes, feelings and behaviours of the underfunctioning partner (the one who is more passive and usually follows the other's lead), as much as the underfunctioning partner shapes those of the overfunctioning partner. Couples become stuck in their own self-reinforcing interactional loops. This position is often self-maintained. Partners have a tendency to reciprocate or respond to negative actions with negative actions of their own. Once one or both partners become downhearted in the relationship, a self-perpetuating process tends to justify the ongoing negative response. On the other hand, when partners embark to interact in a more favourable way with each other, affirmative reciprocity can help to maintain and increase relationship satisfaction, and call forth more assuring and constructive behaviour from the other partner. These cycles of interaction generate stability and affirmation, and leave the couple in a secure place.

This dance of wounds happens something like this: one partner may become emotionally distant because s/he is fearful and critical of others, especially in an intimate relationship with parents and now with a partner. S/he therefore becomes withdrawn and hurt, and may show this distance by acting angry and resentful. Soon the other partner, seeing only these negative loops of anger, organizes his or her responses in terms of making demands for change and, until sufficient changes are made, becomes less easy to please. People who demand change from their partners dig themselves into a deeper and deeper hole as both partners circle around this loop of hurt and anger. Thus both partners become super vigilant and distant. Neither partner decides to exit the system, yet neither can attain the security and intimacy they hope for in a couple relationship.

Soon the couple is locked into the dance of wounds. These hurt feelings can turn into angry criticism, but anger, in this case, is only an attempt to modify the partner's behaviour. **Anger can be seen as a protest against the inflexibility and perceived mean-spiritedness of the partner. In other words, it is only a fight for the love they really are seeking, but all gets lost in the negative dance of wounds.** The dance of wounds is a power struggle, nay, a struggle for survival, fuelled by the fear of loss. One person fears that if they lose the other's love and partnership, they will lose a whole lot of themselves. Often, in therapy, couples tell me how frustrated and resentful they feel about allowing themselves to be so affected by what their partner might say and do. They feel they have very little power over their partner's pushing their buttons.

Example I: John and Margaret's Story

John and Margaret have been married for six years and come into therapy complaining of marital distance and conflict. They say that communication has broken down. John complains that Margaret is distant and spends all her time either at work or in front of the TV. Margaret says that John is critical of anything she tries to do in the relationship. Attempts to talk things through just end in accusations against each other. On the cluster of attachment patterns, Margaret is a strong avoidant person, very individualistic and afraid of intimacy. John has a strong need for attention. He has a distant relationship with his family of origin and seems to overcompensate with his preoccupation with a relationship with Margaret. The following script is a familiar pattern of their fights.

Margaret	John
Why are you always so critical of me, like you were this morning?	You never show me enough attention.
Take this morning, for example. You got on my case for reading the newspaper.	
	Well, when I got up, you never even said good morning.
That is because you don't even touch me anymore at night.	
	How can I touch you when you never say a loving word to me?
It's hard to be nice to you when you are so cold.	
	You're cold! All you do all evening is watch TV and ignore me.
Well, it's a lot better than being criticized by you.	
	You come home from work late, and hardly talk to me.
When I try to talk to you, it is only blame.	
	I just want more attention from you.
I just want you to be nicer to me.	
	Well, you started it.
No, you did.	

"The hole in the sidewalk"

Example II: Beverly and Patrick's Story

Beverly (35) and Patrick (46) have been together for six years and have a four-year-old daughter. Beverly left home when she was 17, stating that she was left out and uncared for in her family. She headed east to work and quickly met and lived with Fred. Within the year she left him and lived with Jim for almost ten years. During most of those years, she felt alone and unhappy. Although she sounds very individuated, in fact Beverly feels quite insecure in relationships and tends to cling to her partner. This is Patrick's first marriage, although he had had several girlfriends. He describes himself as an easygoing man who is close to his family of origin and loves his work. He has a cottage next to his parents' home. Although he sounds comfortable with his relationship with his parents, Patrick is fearful of too much togetherness and is avoidant with Beverly. Beverly and Patrick met and were married within five months. The following script is a common exchange when the dance of wounds is on, but note that his need for avoiding a fight and her need for attention are not being met.

Patrick	Beverly
	I need you to spend more time with me and our daughter.
I have so much to do, fixing the house and the cottage.	
	You and your damn cottage! I am sick and tired of working on it. We are never home.
You always used to love to go there. Remember how you would help me when we were first married?	
	I did that for a while. Now I need you to spend time with me. You always go there.
Not always, just when there is a family gathering.	
	That is twice a month! I get sick when I think of all we did there.
You are never happy with my family!	
	All you think about is them!
There is no pleasing you, is there?	
	You don't care about me at all.
Oh, what's the use!	

"The hole in the sidewalk"

Example III: Paul and Paulette's Story

Paul and Paulette have been married for ten years. Paul, the eldest of four children, left home at the age of 16 to "get out of the house" and away from his angry father. He lived alone for years before getting married. He describes himself as quiet; he also reveals that he is distant from his family and has few friends. Paul avoids all fights yet he never forgets when someone has hurt him. Paulette is the youngest of three children, also from a family where Dad was verbally and physically abusive, but Paulette describes herself as the one who "stood up to Dad." Although she is a "fighter," Paulette doesn't care what others think of her. Neither Paul's need for appeasing nor Paulette's need for "the truth" were getting met in this fight. Their dance of wounds looks something like the following:

Paul	Paulette
Why did you tell my sister that she was too bossy?	
	Someone has to tell the truth around here.
You could have just left it alone.	
	When anyone tells me how to discipline my son, it is my business.
You could have told her in a nicer voice.	
	She was yelling, too.
I hate it when you have to tell everyone what to do.	
	Why don't you stand up for yourself?
You're impossible! I'm getting out of here.	
	Run again! Go ahead! Leave!
I'm going out and won't be back for supper.	
	You can cook your own supper, if you want one.

"The hole in the sidewalk"

This dance of wounds, these circular loops of hurt and anger, only make couples dizzy; it is crazy-making behaviour. All these scripts are really varying formats of a tragic play that gets lived out all too often in couple relationships. The couple has fallen into a state of automatic emotional interactions with rigidly organized responses. The dance of wounds becomes so familiar that partners know only too well where it is going to lead and the automatic fight that will ensue. Once an accustomed communication becomes a regular part of their interaction, couples often assume that, despite further bold attempts to change it, all will continue to be lost. The couple has fallen into their deep hole in the sidewalk, and neither party can see the way out. Attempts to try harder are only repetitions of the same old pattern. Repeated attempts to change the other, overcome the distance, or pretend the damage isn't there are futile. The hurt of this repetitive dance soon turns to anger, and the blame is usually focused on the other person, complete with pointing fingers and shouts of "It's your fault!" Most people react to the threatened loss of love in some form of a childish temper tantrum, perhaps recalling their childhood days when Mom and Dad were likewise seemingly mean and withholding love.

This breach of a love relationship is an unconscious reminder of deficits in a person's experience of parental love, just as the original attachment couples have is often a re-creation of attachment patterns with parents. This is one of the main crisis points in couple relationships, for unless a couple can see their way beyond this repetitive and defensive wall, one partner's hurt too often turns to anger and can add up to couple disaster and separation. **It appears to both partners that the basic problem lies with the other's seeming change of personality, in his/her denial or withholding of love, or worse, their deliberate and unforgiving meanness. "Why have you changed?** Where is that old you that I used to love so much? Come out, come out, wherever you are!"

What is going on here is, in fact, the dance of wounds, probably unconscious at this early stage. Family-of-origin pre-existent wounds are playing in the relationships; as a result, needs and expectations are left unfulfilled, love feels deprived and the closeness that accompanied that "falling-in-love" feeling has gone out the window. Usually at this stage, neither partner is mindful enough to stop the dance and take a time out to see what is going on between them, let alone to become aware of their own contribution to the problem or recognize their own steps in the dance of wounds.

The Same Old Darn Thing

In many ways the dance of wounds is doing the same old darn thing with your partner that you used to do with your parents. The dance of wounds is a recurring and predictable pattern of interactions and conflicts. Attachment theory is intergenerational, especially in regard to assessing and predicting adult attachment patterns based on what people experienced as children. Children tend unconsciously to identify with parents and adopt the same patterns of behaviour that they experienced during childhood. Thus, these patterns of interaction are transmitted more or less faithfully from one generation to the next. These are the sins of the forefathers and foremothers that are passed on to the next generation unless the dance of wounds is re-created into a dance of love.

Past parental attachment behaviours can be transferred to present partner relationships. To put it the other way around, present relationship patterns can be better understood by uncovering experiences or "working models" of childhood and characteristics of past attachment figures, especially parents. This is done by observing, researching and realizing the "unfinished business" of childhood that still organizes present interactional and communication patterns. Clients' current and past family-of-origin climate can be predictive of present couple attachment styles.

Family systems theory states that interactional patterns are reproduced from generation to generation because it is within the family context that most of us learn how to love, communicate and parent. Levels of individuation and intimacy within the family of origin are reproduced in our current relationship with our spouse and significant others. Such interactions and communication ways are what each of us brings to the development of couple relationships, for better or for worse. These old family rules of communication, these old ways of doing things, seem normal enough to us because we have been using them since birth. They can usher us into trouble, however, when we meet and interact with other people, especially an intimate partner, who just happens to have grown up with quite different family rules. It is at these times that the waters of relationship get muddied and tested. Indeed, some people keep repeating the pattern from partner to partner. I have heard it said often enough in therapy how a daughter hated her father so much, she went out and married someone just like him. Similarly, a quiet and withdrawn man may marry a woman who is talkative and extroverted, later to feel the pain of her endless chatter. He leaves her, only to find and marry another woman of similar character.

It seems to be common sense to observe that if our attempts to change this dance and improve it have not worked in the past, it would be well to stop doing what we have been doing and to switch to new behaviours and try other approaches to couple interaction that might work better. To achieve maturity, both partners need to balance individuation and intimacy in the couple relationship.

Pushing Your Buttons

"Watch it! You're pushing my buttons!" is often one of the opening lines in the ongoing dance of wounds. In fact, wounds are emotional buttons. Like the buttons found in elevators, when these emotional buttons are pushed, we react with emotional reactivity that can range from accelerating up to the top floor of anger, or down to the basement of depression. Each of us has a few emotional buttons, born in our family of origin and operative in our present relationship with our partner. **Buttons, like wounds, can be words, tones, facial expressions or bodily gestures that elicit an automatic emotional response ranging from frustration and anger to withdrawal and depression.** Buttons are almost automatic, instinctual and expeditious reactions to old learned family-of-origin interactions. When it comes to buttons, we can respond with a synchronicity of defensive reactions that come out of some unconscious childhood place.

One client said that when his wife would wag her index finger at him to indicate that he was "a bad boy," he was instantly reminded of the countless times that his mother used the same finger to lecture him about something he was doing. That "finger button" raised in him sadness, hurt, frustration, guilt and often anger. Another client spoke of a certain tone her husband would use in a confrontation, a tone that reminded her of her father's condescending voice when she was young, and of all she could not do right. For one female client, the button was her husband's reaching for and having just one beer; it brought her back to the days of her father's drinking and accompanying anger. For one male client, his button was about needing to almost purposely fail or mess up when confronted by his wife's perfectionism, for it reminded him of his father's constant words to him that he would "never be any good at anything."

Buttons are those places in the recesses of our primarily unconscious emotional gut where old family-of-origin wounds reside. These wounds await the call by seemingly loving partners to come forward and express themselves in ways that are repetitive and equivalent to our reactions during childhood. **To know our buttons, and develop new ways of reacting to them and working with them, is the beginning of the end of the dance of wounds.**

Hurt and Anger

In a real sense, hurt and anger are one and the same button. If you hurt me, I will get angry; if you distance yourself from me, I will be indignant; if you make too many demands of me and my time, and I feel smothered, I will become incensed. Anger is a natural response to hurt; these emotions are two sides of the same coin. On the other hand, if I feel angry, or see anger in my partner, I now also know there must be hurt present. My partner's anger is a sign or symptom of some hurt present in our relationship. As partners who dance the dance of wounds, we now have two choices: we can chase down the anger and respond with more anger, or we can ask about the hurt and be curious about what may be hurtful for our partner. Talking about and pursuing the hurts rather than fighting with our anger is an entirely different conversation and a conscious moving away from the dance of wounds.

Example: Responding to Anger

The first partner has an angry outburst:

Partner 1: "You make me so angry! You just don't care about me at all! You never show me any affection!"

Compare the following two replies:

Partner 2 (pursuing the anger): "You are the one who always gets mad! Just listen to yourself for a minute!"

Partner 2 (pursuing the hurt): "Maybe there is some hurt here. I'm sorry if I hurt you."

The Dance of Wounds Is Also a Call for Growth

Now that the cat is out of the bag and we see our relationship shattered into a thousand pieces on the floor, it is decision time: do we work to save the relationship or do we cash in our chips and separate? A popular book encourages us to feel the fear and do it anyway. Perhaps a friend can become a facilitator to suggest we look at what is happening to us as a couple. An article in the newspaper or a therapist will ask us to think about what we are doing. However this "coming to our senses" happens, we can turn this crisis into an opportunity. This might be a necessary and fortunate conflict that is calling us to a deeper sense of intimacy. How can we move from this dance of wounds, which inadvertently or unconsciously holds us in a negative interaction cycle, to a dance of re-creation, which enables us to create new perceptions and responses for each other in the direction of a positive spiral?

Intimate relationships, we have suggested, are repetitions of our attachment patterns with our parents, for better and for worse. These relationships bring out both the healthy and the unhealthy ways of relating and loving we learned in childhood. As the honeymoon comes to an end and the veil of illusion falls away, the dance of wounds moves into high gear. This can be a wonderful opportunity for partners to examine and work on unfinished business and unresolved family-of-origin issues. The very things that attracted them to each other in the first place are now bringing about this breach of relationship. Turning the dance of wounds into a call for growth and change will help both of them to address and heal old family-of-origin and unfinished attachment wounds.

Any call for growth and change needs to be, first and foremost, a call to look at and change ourselves. When we become a better person, and we can secure a better self-understanding, we also become a better mate and lover for our partner. In fact, it is often one partner who initially begins the journey towards healing the relationship, and often I see just one partner in therapy. The journey to re-creating the relationship can begin when one partner starts to model and work on herself or himself, and hopes and waits for the other to catch on. This will be the topic of the next chapter. There is hope for wounded relationships, and love can be re-discovered and increased to deeper and fresher dimensions.

Exercise: The Dance of Wounds

This exercise is designed to help you as a couple notice and trace the steps each of you does in the dance of wounds. Sketching the steps on paper will allow you to become more observant about their dance.

Things you say and do (words, tone, facial expressions or body language) that make me feel safe and loved are...

1)

2)

3)

Things you say and do (words, tone, facial expressions or body language) that activate my wounds and push my buttons are...

1)

2)

3)

If I were to track our dance of wounds, it might look something like this:

He said   **She said**

PART II:
THE DANCE OF RE-CREATING RELATIONSHIPS

6
Re-creating the Relationship I:
Know Thyself

I walk down the same street.
　　There is a deep hole in the sidewalk.
　　I see it there.
　　I still fall in ... it's a habit ... but
　　　　My eyes are open
　　　　I know where I am.
It's my fault.
I get out immediately
　　　　—*Portia Nelson, "Autobiography in Five Short Chapters"*

You must be the change you wish to see in the world.
　　　　—*Mohandas K. Gandhi*

Every failure to cope with a life situation must be laid, in the end, to a restriction of consciousness. Wars and temper tantrums are the makeshifts of ignorance. Regrets are illuminations come too late.
　　　　—Anonymous

No one can bless any other
until (s)he can bless his/her own origins.
　　　　—*Carlyle Marney*

Know Thyself

"Know thyself" are the wise and guiding words of Socrates. "Physician, heal thyself," proclaims Jesus, citing an old proverb. The only way to truly change the world, writes Gandhi, is to change yourself. This is true of changing our partner as well. The word *buddha* means to wake up, to know, to understand and to love. Deep inside, we all want to be honest and contented with ourselves. After all, we will never really be fulfilled anywhere, with anyone, nor will others be satisfied with us, if we are not satisfied with ourselves. If we are no good for ourselves, we will be no good for anyone else. There must be joy within us before we can give joy to others. The journey to love and fulfillment in life begins with an understanding of ourselves. From this follows the direction our lives will take. This self-insight is one of the main criteria of maturity. Self-insight is the ability to accept our disagreeable as well as our desirable qualities, together with a sense of humour that precludes affectation and helps maintain a sense of proportion. It is wise to keep a sense of humour about ourselves; after all, everyone else probably has a decent sense of humour about us! Perhaps nothing requires greater intellectual heroism than the willingness to see ourselves in the mirror. The process of loving others begins with knowing ourselves, and includes steps like loving ourselves, being thoughtful and taking personal responsibility for ourselves.

Einstein reminds us that problems cannot be solved at the same level of consciousness in which they were created. In other words, partners cannot solve couple problems by staying at the same level of self-awareness, the same level of interaction. Someone will have to start looking at the issues from different perspectives and with an open curiosity about the development of these couple issues. Couples will have to go to a different place and to a new way of thinking and seeing their problems together. Beginning the journey of re-creating distant or broken relationships will demand a different and deeper route for each partner. The best place to start is with a new and fresh look at ourselves: we must become more conscious about who we are and how we interact with others, especially those we love. Stupidity is thinking that if I try the same thing for the thousand and first time, the result will be different from the previous thousand times I tried.

Most couples come into my therapy office and begin their conversation with the word "You!" Their finger is usually pointing at their partner. "It is all your fault" are common words in the opening minutes of couple therapy, along with "You have got to change." But remember: when we point a finger at someone else, we are also pointing three fingers back at ourselves. Looking within is a good place to start searching for fault and real changes.

This is not easy to do. We may not say that we are perfect, but parts of us are excellent, and it is so much easier to look at our partner's faults and foibles than our own. **But we need to take responsibility for our contribution to any problem or issues in the relationship.** Most partners tend to ignore their own starring role in the couple conflict and prefer to focus on the flaws of their partner. We are very knowledgeable and certain of their problems, wounds and inadequacies, but we have a difficult time seeing our own. In fact, when we are most unhappy and dissatisfied with ourselves, we tend to place undue demands and expectations onto our partner, trying to get our partner to do and say those things that will make us feel better, to make us feel more emotionally secure. Our wounds are born within our family of origin, and we need to take responsibility for how we will integrate these wounds. If there is to be love on earth, it has to begin with us.

Example: Taking Responsibility

In the movie *Dead Poets' Society* (Tom Schulman, 1989), Todd is sent to the boarding school where his popular older brother was valedictorian. Todd's roommate, Neil, although exceedingly bright and popular, is very much under the thumb of his overbearing father. The two boys, along with their classmates, meet the wise and inspiring Professor Keating, who encourages them to individuate, to "seize the day" and live their own lives. Each, in their own way, follows this path of individuation from their family of origin, and is changed for life. The enmeshment between Neil and his father is a classic struggle for individuation gone wrong. His dad is trying to relive his own teenage years through his son. Neil tries to impress his father, but realizes Dad wants him to be someone he is not. Dad forbids Neil to become an actor, tells him he is taking him out of the school, and plans to send him to military school and then to Harvard to study medicine. That same night, Neil ends his life. The movie ends with people passing blame around; no one will take responsibility. Parents' own immaturity and poor self-awareness are usually passed onto their children, at times with tragic results. The sins of the fathers and mothers are passed down to the children, most often because of the parents' own unhealed wounds, sometimes as sheer evil.

Studying Our Family of Origin

In order to know ourselves better and become more objective observers of ourselves as we are present in our relationship with our partner, we need to study ourselves, especially within the context of our family of origin. We need to become a researcher of our own family-of-origin dynamics, watching as we enter into and participate in significant love relationships within our family of origin and within our relationship with our partner. We need to be able to see what we are doing, and to think about what makes us do what we do. We all want to understand "why" we are as we are, doing what we are doing. We also need to be aware of our feelings while present with our partner.

Chapter 1 pointed out that it is within our family of origin that our wounds were born, and that these wounds continue to operate in some way within our relationship with our partner today. Childhood wounds tend to drive most relationships, as family-of-origin wounds are re-enacted with adult partners. A family-of-origin review helps us to see and uncover patterns and characteristics of our lives that inform us about who we are now, and how our strengths and wounds dance with our partner's. Doing family-of-origin work helps to resolve past wounds in the current relationship, for knowledge of these past wounds brings better insight and differentiation to our present relationships. Likewise, our present relationship with our partner can bring knowledge and healing to our family-of-origin wounds. Just as we need to balance individuation and intimacy, so too we need to bring balance to past and present.

Doing family-of-origin work is difficult. It means not only taking a good look at ourselves and our experiences of growing up within our family, but it probably also means going home to visit with parents and siblings and opening a door of dialogue with them so that we may better understand ourselves and see our wounds more clearly. It means digging in the dirt of the past, and uncovering feelings and hurts that may be forgotten (although not really) or, at least, best left alone. We have to remember that objects in the rearview mirror are closer than they appear: in other words, doing family-of-origin work will bring up many feelings and memories that may not have been processed properly. On the other hand, by reviewing and filling out the stories of our family of origin and by checking out family rumours and grapevines, we can become our own best therapist and researcher and begin the process of rewriting our relationship scripts. In doing so, we become a fly on the wall that hears and sees all that we do, an internal camera that captures our words, actions and emotions and plays them back so we can observe and know ourselves and live these things in the here and now according to our own choosing. **We review the movie that is our lives and pick out some highlights of our script, becoming more aware of how we can change the storyline from what it was to what we want it to be now.** As a result, we begin to see ourselves as our partner sees us, or to have the courage to ask good friends to be honest with us about how they experience us. We can ask our partner, who is usually more than happy to tell us what problems they see in us. Even more courageous would be to ask for feedback from people who don't really like us. It takes courage to admit and grapple with our wounds and move to make changes in ourselves.

Family Maps

How can we better understand ourselves, especially the family-of-origin experiences in which our wounds and attachment pattern was born, and become more active players in our own healing? Bowen encourages us to make a research project out of our lives and relationships, to take increasing responsibility for knowing ourselves and the dynamics of our families of origin. One way to do this research on your own family is to make your family map, or genogram. Family maps are descriptive pictures or graphic portrayals of our family, including members, roles, relationships, gifts and wounds. The family map is a history of the flow of emotional processes through the family generations. It is a visual image of who you are, reflecting family patterns: a picture method of taking, storing and processing relationship information. It is a relatively simple, non-intrusive, easily updated tool that provides a quick reference for complex patterns of relationships. As such, it can be used as a source of self-knowledge and self-awareness about gifts and wounds.

The family map can help reveal memories of childhood relationships with parents, together with current partner attachment patterns, and can delineate recurring relationship patterns. Researching your own family of origin can be done over several years, as you gain more and more information during visits with parents, uncles and aunts, or cousins. Old family stories lead to hypotheses and further knowledge and understanding of family history. Partners can be outside experts on your family for they stand as more neutral observers of how you interact with your family of origin. What you are looking for in a family map is your attachment pattern in intimate relationships, an attachment pattern that was developed in your family of origin, that continues in the couple relationship, and that will probably be passed on to your children.

Basic Genogram Format

Male ☐   Female ○   Birthdate [1949│2049]   Death date

Marriage (give date)
Husband on left, wife on right — m.1996

Living together — L.T.1995

Marital separation (give date) — m.96 / 97

Divorce (give date) — m.96 s. / 97 // 98

Children: List in birth order;
begin with oldest on the left — m.96 97│98│99│00

Adopted or
foster children

Family with four children — 80│83│84│89

Fraternal twins

Identical twins

Pregnancy — 3 months

Spontaneous abortion

Induced abortion — X

Stillbirth

Husband with several wives — m.55 // d.59 │ m.60 // d.70 │ m.80 / s.83

Two partners who had previous marriages — m.72 // d.76 │ m.03 │ m.73 // d.76 │ m.80 // d.94

Type of relationship
Very close relationship / enmeshed ═══════

Conflictual relationship ∿∿∿

Distant relationship - - - - - - - -

Estranged or cut off ——┤ ├——

Enmeshed and conflictual ⩨⩨⩨

Figure I shows the main elements of the family map. Begin by drawing your basic family structure, including father, mother and siblings. A family map should cover at least three generations, including grandparents on both parents' side. Include names, dates of births (ages can be placed inside the person's circle or square) and deaths. Also include cohabitations, marriages, separations and divorces, and the dates of these. Maps can include information such as each person's levels of education, health and addictions history, and other significant information. Family rules can also be noted.

The construction of the family map can reveal attachment patterns, whether enmeshed or cut-off, or the attachment possibilities that lie between these two. In couple relationships, after making their family maps, each partner can then understand their own and their partner's attachment pattern, begin to know and accept themselves, and understand and appreciate possible couple differences. Repetitive patterns of functioning suggest the possibility of these attachment patterns continuing in the present and into the future. Reciprocal and cyclical relationship patterns can be represented, and responses to questions of intimacy can be analyzed to identify intimacy patterns of the couple and the rules and assumptions related to intimacy.

Family maps are fairly easy to draw. To guide you in the construction, I will draw the family maps of Joe and Mary, whose story was presented at the beginning of Chapter I. A good place to begin is with your own nuclear family of you and your partner and any children you may have. For example, Joe and Mary have known each other for eleven years, lived together for five years and been married for two years. They have no children.

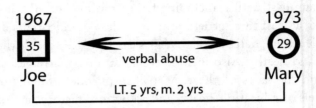

I need assurance
wants more hugs and affection
perfectionist
fears new things
phones mom every day
fast temper

left home at age 17
capable/independent
"Don't touch me"
family negotiator
angry/yells a lot
depressed/impatient

Turning our attention to Mary's family of origin, we note that Mary is the middle of three children, with an older brother and younger sister. Some key information is noted. Her older brother is "out of it," dysfunctioning on drugs and doing jail time. Mary's younger sister is the "good girl." Mary's mother and father are described using Mary's own words. Your family of origin can go back to your grandparents and uncles and aunts.

passionate
funny
gone/worked away
alcoholic
verbally abusive
mean/scary

loving
sweet
passive
not speak up
fear to confront

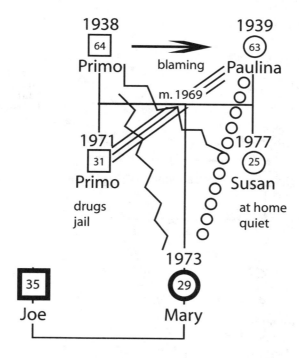

Joe's family of origin is depicted in a similar fashion. Joe is the younger of two children, with an older sister who moved away from home to attend university and who "never comes home." Joe's parents are described using Joe's own words; Mary was more than happy to contribute some descriptors as well. In constructing a couple's family map, partners are often better observers of their partner's family of origin as they are more distant and, at times, more objective.

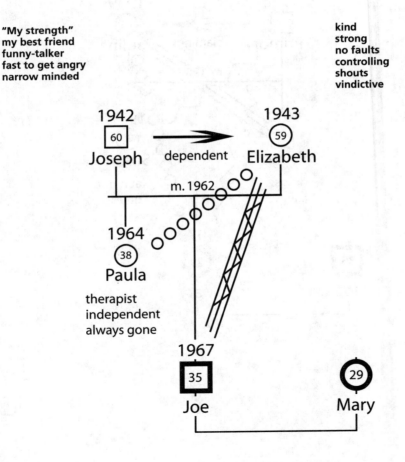

"My strength"
my best friend
funny-talker
fast to get angry
narrow minded

kind
strong
no faults
controlling
shouts
vindictive

1942
60
Joseph   dependent   Elizabeth
1943
59

m. 1962

1964
38
Paula

therapist
independent
always gone

1967
35
Joe   Mary   29

As you construct your own map, observe and write down felt memory words that come to your mind for significant others, especially your parents. You can begin by enumerating three to five "nice" descriptor words that come to mind when you, especially as a child between the ages of five and ten, remember your father and mother. Then identify three to five "not-so-nice" words for your mother and father. You can do a similar exercise for all your siblings and significant others who lived with you as a child, such as a grandparent or a long-time visitor. Carefully observe both the words and the feelings these words evoke as you add them to your family map. These descriptor words can reveal certain attachment and family interactional patterns, which can be written in as shown in the following figure. In fact, these words describe the attachment patterns of significant people in the genogram. When this exercise was done for Mary and Joe's families of origin, the following family map emerged.

Figure 5

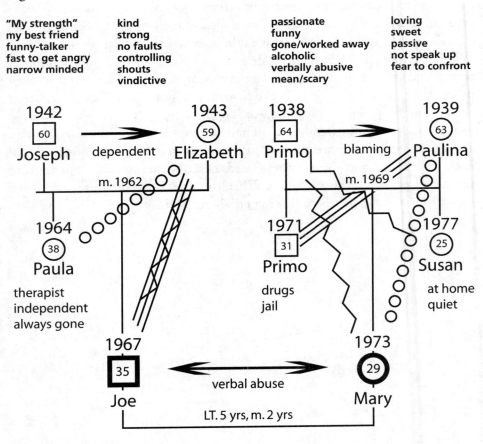

"My strength"
my best friend
funny-talker
fast to get angry
narrow minded

kind
strong
no faults
controlling
shouts
vindictive

passionate
funny
gone/worked away
alcoholic
verbally abusive
mean/scary

loving
sweet
passive
not speak up
fear to confront

1942 [60] Joseph — dependent → 1943 (59) Elizabeth

1938 [64] Primo — blaming → 1939 (63) Paulina

m. 1962

m. 1969

1964 (38) Paula

therapist
independent
always gone

1971 [31] Primo

drugs
jail

1977 (25) Susan

at home
quiet

1967 [35] Joe ←— verbal abuse —→ 1973 (29) Mary

LT. 5 yrs, m. 2 yrs

I need assurance
wants more hugs and affection
perfectionist
fears new things
phones mom every day
fast temper

left home at age 17
capable/independent
"Don't touch me"
family negotiator
angry/yells a lot
depressed/impatient

Partners with a *secure/differentiated* attachment pattern tend to describe their relationship with their parents as consistently responsive, in that their parents were "always there for me." These parents had a good sense of personal identity and communicated a positive view of themselves and their children to others. As a result, secure/differentiated partners are "easy to get close to" because they have a good balance between how they express their autonomy and their connectedness with others. These partners value attachment and can realistically talk about it.

Partners with an *enmeshed/preoccupied* attachment pattern tend to describe their relationship with their parents as erratic and inconsistent, a sort of "there now, gone tomorrow" uncertainty. These parents tend to hold a negative view of themselves and have low self-esteem while holding a positive view of others in the sense of needing them. These parents show less love but they are not rejecting. Enmeshed/preoccupied partners often complain that they had to fight for parental attention. Such partners engage in a confusing discussion regarding their relationship, often presenting in a passive and/or angry way. They exhibit strong dependency that can present as caregiving. Their usual complaint against their partner is that they "are reluctant to get as close as I would like." These adults are still caught in old interactional patterns and tend to be clingy partners.

Partners with an *avoidant/cut-off* attachment pattern often describe parents as unresponsive and non-present. These parents tend to be rejecting, distant, withdrawn and away a lot. They hold a negative view of the world, often insinuating that they are self-sufficient. Avoidant/cut-off partners tend to be highly independent and invulnerable, and they can deny the need for close relationships. In a sense, they seem detached from feelings and are uncomfortable being too close to others. These partners downplay the importance of intimacy in their relationships.

The process and feelings attached to the experience of finding these words are revealing. Some people are hesitant to say anything — nice or not so nice. Others can't find the words. For some, speaking the words can bring forth feelings of pride and love; for others, these words evoke feelings of pain or hurt.

All these can reveal attachment patterns ranging from enmeshed to secure to cut-off. You can review the pathways of attachment patterns in Chapter I to locate your own more accurately. Some caution and practical judgment are needed here. You may be uncomfortable talking about your parents. You may feel you are blaming your parents, or be afraid to identify yourself before a partner with whom you are having conflict. On the other hand, your partner can be very helpful in observing your attachment patterns within your family of origin, as he or she probably has a more objective point of view.

A second line of family map questions tries to uncover your space and place within the family system. Where did you fit in your father's or mother's affections? Who was Mom's and Dad's favourite child when you were five to ten years old? Who were you closest to? Mom? Dad? Sibling? Other? None? How would you describe your relationship pattern with your father? With your mother? With your sibling(s)? What were your alliances? Who were your favourites? Whose team were you on as a child? Answers to these questions can point towards a specific attachment pattern.

In the case of Joe and Mary, we see that Joe was his mom's favourite child. The two of them were highly enmeshed, needing to phone each other almost daily to be in touch. In a real sense, Joe had not yet left home emotionally, and this was one of the main causes of couple conflict. On the other hand, Mary left home too young and too fast, and has continued her avoidant/cut-off relationship with her parents. Joe and Mary approach their own couple relationship from opposite ends of the pathways of attachment patterns.

Family maps provide a wide focus, a multigenerational look at who we are individually and as a couple. Because they are on paper, these maps can become a more objective expression of how both partners see themselves and each other. The object of the exercise is not to argue who is right but to "know thyself" better, with as much openness and honesty as both partners can muster. At the same time, direction for growth and change is indicated. Joe needs to move in the direction of more individuation from his parents, especially his mother. Mary has to move in the direction of further togetherness or reconnectedness with her parents. Maturity or the secure/differentiated attachment style is a balance of togetherness and individuation, a better coming together of both aspects of a healthy relationship with more equilibrium.

Example: George's Story

George was a young man in his final year of a business administration program. He presented himself in therapy with a moderate degree of depression. He was doing well in classes, and he was very satisfied with his relationship with his girlfriend. All of life seemed open for him, but he was very unhappy. George said he was unhappy because he was on a business track but he really wanted to play music. George had no real reason for not following his desired music career. During the genogram construction, George stated that, as the firstborn son, he was destined to take over his father's business. His father, also a firstborn son, had taken over the business from his father. A family rule was operating here, and George felt compelled to fall into line. It took some time for George to gather the courage to tell his father that he did not want to go into the family business, but wished to follow a music career. When he did communicate this to his parents, his depression began to lift.

Our Contribution to the Problem

As we come to know ourselves better, and in deeper ways, we need to move on to the next question. How aware are we of our contribution to the couple problem? Do we really know and appreciate the effects our own wounds have on the hopes, feelings and sensitivity of our partner? Have we seen how our wound is dancing with our partner's wound, and vice versa? To know and name our wound is to identify one part of the couple problem and to move in the direction of a solution. **Can we begin our dialogue with our partner with the word "I," and initiate a conversation about ourselves: what we see, what we feel, what we want or do not want, and especially, what our contribution to the couple problem might be?** We need to keep the emphasis on ourselves and what we know about ourselves, to observe and know our own childhood tapes or blueprint of behaviours and name them for who we really are. At the same time, we must let our partner see who we really are, and let our partner know that often we are reacting out of our wounds and not out of meanness, as partners often assume. Knowing and acknowledging our contribution to our couple problem is the beginning of healing and, in a real way, this sort of truth will help set us free as a couple.

This Is My Wound: Help Me

When therapy begins and partners are pointing fingers at each other in a blaming mode, it takes a lot of work to move that couple into a more differentiated stance where they can begin talking about themselves and taking responsibility for their own actions. "You" statements are dangerous and unproductive in couple therapy. "I" statements are the beginning of couple healing. **To name our wound, claim our wound and heal our wound by being aware of it and how it functions in the couple relationship is the dawning of insight and movement towards a more mature/secure/differentiated attachment pattern.**

One of the definitions of love in a couple relationship is trust and willingness to be very open and honest with your partner, especially about your own wounds and how they might be dancing in the relationship. It is a big act of love to say to your partner: **"This is my wound: please help me."** This short sentence speaks volumes about the work you are doing to "know thyself." This knowledge helps you filter your present behaviour and words through the lenses of your own family-of-origin learning and recognize wounds that you now want to work with and heal.

Example: Kelly's Story

One of my clients, Kelly, shared the following recollection of a family dance recital.

I do believe that both my parents lived out of their wounds, as we all do, the best they knew how with their own family-of-origin music they were taught. For the most part, their whole symphony was off-key. They were tone deaf! I hated their tune. In time, there were steps and patterns in their dance of wounds that I began to recognize. Their struggle of who would lead the dance, the stepping on toes, the full-blown warfare in which we kids would get dragged into choosing sides, and the retaliation which often included us kids as pawns and dealmakers. The music would finally stop and the dance of silence would begin: sometimes they were really stockpiling new weapons of mass accusation.

Sometimes there was a truce or a disarming. Then, after hours or days, the dance would resume – the steps were of victory and power, with my mother usually being the conductor and my defeated father dancing to her music again. At times the melody would change slightly: sometimes it was a waltz, sometimes a quickstep, often a frenzy with no unison, no rhyme or reason. The steps may have varied but the tune never changed. As eldest daughter, I tried to keep the other kids off the dance floor as much as I could.

Finally my mother went on to dance with another partner, packing her bags with the same old tune. She developed new variations of the old tune with her new partner; their dance of wounds looked much the same as before. My father was not capable of life without his dance-of-wounds partner and drank himself to death. Over time, all us kids left this dysfunctional home but, for the most part, we brought the dance along to practise with our own partners.

So how can we help ourselves and let our partner help us heal our wounds? The second part of this book deals with the answer to this question in several ways: it encourages you to know yourself, to communicate with your partner, to establish a safe emotional connection, and to forgive yourself for what you might have done out of these wounds, especially with your partner. **I believe that more often than not, partners are not acting out of deliberate meanness or vindictiveness when there is conflict within a couple relationship. Rather,**

they act out of unredeemed wounds. Part of the admission of "This is my wound: please help me!" is to give ourselves a break and let go of our own self-doubts and self-criticisms. It is often easier to forgive others than to forgive ourselves, but it is hard to move into a new and better future if we are still holding guilt and shame from our past. Since our eyes are now open to the hole in our sidewalk of life, we need to use our energy to move ahead and find new ways of creating a more loving relationship with our partner.

Personal Authority

We are each the author of ourselves, of our own individual stories. We have the authority to create our personal life as we want to live it. Since life is the place for the performance of our story, what particular story do we want others, especially our partner, to know about us? What authority within us enables us to dream, script and act a meaningful narrative that can become the chronicle of who we are and how we want to be known by others? Bowen calls someone who undertakes this task the "differentiated person." Bowlby refers to them as the "secure person." Williamson describes them as the "person with personal authority." This is the goal of the work of healing our wound.

Personal authority is a sense of peerhood for us as adult children with our parents. It suggests that we need to become "friends" with our parents – equals on the journey of life. Williamson states that personal authority is a pattern of abilities to do the following:

1) to order and direct one's own thoughts and opinions;
2) to choose to express or not to express one's thoughts and opinions regardless of social pressures;
3) to make and respect one's personal judgments to the point of regarding these judgments as justification for action;
4) to take responsibility for the totality of one's experience in life;
5) to initiate or receive (or decline to receive) intimacy voluntarily, in conjunction with the ability to establish clear boundaries to the self at will; and

6) to experience and relate to all other persons without exception, including "former parents," as peers in the experience of being human.

One of the signs of personal authority is the power and willingness to open up interpersonal communication so that feelings, wants and opinions can be honestly put on the table, whether that is between you and your partner, or with your parents. This is a necessary condition for the healing of interactional wounds to happen. We'll look at this topic in greater detail in the next chapter.

Re-creating Your Relationship with Your Parents

One major place to begin the process of healing our wound is to re-create a better relationship with our parents. Most of us have unfinished business with our parents. Incomplete and strained relationships with parents have a negative effect on all other intimate relationships in our lives. We can rationalize an enmeshed relationship with our parents as "taking care of them," or a cut-off relationship as something that allowed us to live our own lives. No matter how we might try to handle the situation with our parents, if unfinished business, or emotional wounds, or conflicting feelings are still present, they can influence our relationship with our partner. **The three most significant relationships each one of us has is with our parents, with our partner and with our children.** I strongly believe that what we learned from our parents we will practise with our partner – and teach to our children. Therefore, as we learn about ourselves and our own contribution to the dance of wounds, there are good reasons to re-create our relationship with our parents at the same time. And it is our job to begin the process. As children, we learned to blame our parents for lots of things, but once we have reached the age of 18 to 25, it is our responsibility to create relationships as we want them, and blame will no longer hold up with our parents. If I want to grow, I need to create relationships that enhance growth and love with all significant people in my life.

We learned attachment patterns and ways of relating within our family of origin, and we bring these interactional patterns to our couple relationships as well as to our parenting of our children. Going home again can help us get in touch with our family-of-origin dynamics, name them and claim them, and then make the changes we really want to make with our parents so that our new relationship better expresses our attachment with them. Changing our relationship with our parents to be more like a relationship of peers helps each of us leave home emotionally and become a better partner. **The degree of mature relationship balance we learned within our family of origin will probably be the way we live the relationship with our partner and pass onto our children.** Seen from a family systems perspective, it is important to note, therefore, that as we change any one of these significant relationships, we are, in fact, enabling ourselves to bring these changes to all the other relationships. As we become aware of and make positive changes in our relationship with our partner, for example, in order to be able to communicate better with less emotional reactivity, we will also be able to do so with our parents and children as well.

We can and need to go home again to bring our relationships with our parents into good order so that we can learn to leave home emotionally, in the complete sense of that word. I firmly believe that parents are waiting for us to come home and talk things out, perhaps even wanting to apologize for their past mistakes so that they, too, can get on with a more mature relationship with their children. This means that we will be able to deal with any guilt and fear learned within our family of origin. It might mean forgiving our parents and letting go of lingering resentments or old grudges or hurts remembered since childhood. Going home to reconstruct a better relationship with parents is not about blaming parents for our wounds, or about disturbing them in their old age. Rather, it is about desiring to have a better and more balanced relationship with them. Moving towards more relationship balance of individuation and intimacy with our parents is one of the better ways to bring about a more balanced relationship with our partner. It does a marriage good to work on improving relationships with parents, since, in the process, we will be addressing and working out the emotional reactions in relationship with our significant other.

Example: Letting a Child Cry

My more difficult parental relationship was with my mom, in part because of her strong personality and her ability to throw around good old Catholic guilt. One early memory I have of her was when I was a young child and Mom had "put me down" on the bed for my afternoon nap. In fact, my felt memory is that I was probably being overly active (again) that day and Mom, who had had enough of me, put me to bed and closed the door. I was crying, feeling alone and unloved. When I shared this story with my mother several years ago, she had no memory of it, but stated that she often felt frustrated with me due to my hyperactivity. Several years later, when my little girl, Paulina, was about 18 months old, she was overly active one day. I put her into her crib for a nap, and she cried. But I had had enough, so I shut the door and left her to cry for a while. As I sat there listening to her, the old memory of my experience with my mother came back to me, and, for the first time, in a depth of feeling, I was able to forgive my mother, for now I understood.

Many therapists encourage people to write a letter to their parents. Below is a form of such a letter I often use with clients. The real purpose of a letter to parents is to make the relationship better. It is not meant to be a dumping ground for hurts and anger. Those feelings need to be taken care of by yourself elsewhere, perhaps with a therapist, so that painful feelings may be dealt with in therapy and not projected onto parents in the letter. The letter is meant to be open, honest, direct and loving. Re-creating your relationship with parents will take time — months or even years. There can be lots of old memories, wounds and emotional reactions to process for both sides. Patience, thoughtfulness and humour are helpful companions. Read and reread your letter until it feels right and truly reflects your desire to make your relationship with your parent(s) better.

Letter to My Parent

Hello

Purpose of the letter

The real purpose of this letter is to make our relationship better. In order to do that, I want to make some changes in our relationship. This letter will try to outline some of the family history as I experienced it, as well as some changes I hope for and why.

Coming up to date

I want to bring you, my parent, up to date as to where I have been, what I have learned about myself (these years, and/or perhaps as a result of therapy) ... some examples.

Thank you

I thank you, Mom / Dad, for some of the good things I can remember that you did / said / loved me for ... some examples.

Regrets

I also want to share with you that, as I prepare for a new future and a new, better and different relationship with you, I need to let go of (and forgive) some old hurts/angers and regrets, for example...

I feel bad that...

It hurt that you did(n't)...

I am angry when I think of...

Questions

In this letter, I want to take the opportunity to ask you about... (anything and everything you always wanted to know about your parent, what they did / said, etc.)

Why did(n't) you...
Where were you when...
How did...

Off the hook as parent

I want to tell you that I no longer need you to be my parent in the sense of being mothering/fathering, and I would like to change our relationship to become that of friends, peers and adult-to-adult family living. I can assure you that I am very able to live as an independent adult and I wish you the best in your life, enjoying it as you see fit.

Personal differentness

I have come to realize that I am similar to and different from you in characteristics, mannerisms, behaviour, attitudes, beliefs, emotions, etc. (some examples)

Changes sought in the relationship

Some changes will need to take place:
I can no longer accept, and therefore need you to stop doing (some examples) ...
I would like and therefore want to ask you to start doing (some examples) ...

To the future

In some senses, the old relationship I had with you is gone. I look forward to being in a new, developing relationship of being friends, peers and family.

Often parents are waiting for adult children to come home and make things right between them; to talk things through and clear the air; to get on with the business of living the future and no longer arguing about the past, whether verbally or silently when one person holds a grudge.

Sample letter to my parent:

Dear Mom,

I am writing you this letter to find ways to make our relationship better. I love you and I want to put our fights behind us and allow us to get to know each other anew as friends. In order to do that, I will review some of the important things I see in our relationship and suggest places where I need to make some changes so that our relationship can become more loving. You might know that I have been looking at my own life quite a bit these past years, in what I read and with the help of my support group and therapy. I feel like I have grown up and changed a lot over this time, and I feel proud of my accomplishments. There is much that I can be thankful to you and Dad for, especially in daring to risk new things. I can see how I am quite a bit like you and Dad.

At the same time, as I prepare for a new and better future with you and Dad, I need to let go of some old hurts. I always had the feeling that you loved my older sister more than you loved me, and that memory still hurts a bit when I see you both together. I feel bad that we had all those fights when I was a teenager, as I tried to find my own place in the family and this world. It seemed like you never really stopped to listen to me at all. I was especially angry when you helped move my sister to university, but you never helped me when I moved into that house with my friends. I would like to feel like you loved me as much. Why did you never stand up to Dad when he was coming down so hard on me, or the times he would hit me? You knew he was drinking and that was not right. Why did you just not leave him? We might have been better off.

But all that is the past, and now I want to get on with a new future. I don't need your approval now as much as I did then. I am well able to look after myself and I hope that we can let the past hurts go. I can see that I am different than my sister, and, in fact, probably more like my dad than her. Maybe that is why you seemed so far away from me for much of my life.

As I seek to re-create my relationship with you, I need to ask that you stop telling me what to do. If you have ideas for me, you are welcome to offer them and I will give them proper consideration. Also, don't ask me where I was last night. I am 28 and I can take care of myself. Just tell me that you hope I had fun. I also ask that you not compare me to my sister or tell me all the "great" things she is doing. I guess that I am really asking that you stop treating me like a little girl and try to become my friend. For example, I like it when you ask about my job, or about what I bought for my new apartment. I also like your stories of when you were my age, even if the times are so different.

Mom, I want a better relationship with you. We both will have to make changes. I want to be able to talk with you as a peer and a friend, and move our relationship into a more adult-adult frame. Thanks for being my mom, and I hope we can work on this over the next while.

Love, Susan

As we shall see in the rest of this book, this dialogue with your parents will require a solid knowledge of yourself, the courage and ability to communicate this with your parents, a sincere desire to connect emotionally and, perhaps, the need to forgive and be forgiven and let go of past hurts. Re-creating your relationship with your parents is part of learning to love others — especially your partner and children — in a more genuine way.

Twelve Commandments of Mental Health
(Taken from Gestalt Therapy)

1. Live in the "now."

2. Live in the "here."

3. Accept yourself as you are.

4. See and interact with your environment as it is, not as you wish it to be.

5. Be honest with yourself.

6. Express yourself in terms of what you want, think, feel, rather than manipulate yourself and others through rationalizations, expectations, judgments or distortions.

7. Express fully the complete range of emotions – the unpleasant as well as the pleasant.

8. Accept no external demands that go contrary to your best knowledge of yourself.

9. Be willing to experiment, to encounter new situations.
10. Be open to change and growth.

11. Keep the memories of the past and concerns for the future in perspective.

12. Use the word "appropriate" as a touchstone for your choices.

Exercise: Know Thyself

The purpose of this exercise is to become aware of and admit your own wounds and contribution to any couple problem you might be having. Note that we each only have a wound or two, and that acknowledging them is vital for couple re-creation.

My wounds, as best I know them now, are

1)

2)

To heal my contribution to our problem, I will change by

Stop Doing   **Start Doing**

1)

2)

3)

7
Re-creating the Relationship II: Communication

I walk down the same street.
> There is a deep hole in the sidewalk.
> I walk around it.
> —*Portia Nelson, "Autobiography in Five Short Chapters"*

Everyone hears only what [s]he understands.
> —*Johann Wolfgang von Goethe (1749–1832)*

People don't get along because they fear each other.
People fear each other because they don't know each other.
They don't know each other because they have not properly
communicated with each other.
> —*Martin Luther King Jr.*

I want you to know me! Please listen. I want to know you! Please talk.
> —*Martin Rovers*

What Is Communication?

Communication is the life blood in the creation, maintenance and growth of couple relationships. It brings the necessary oxygen, nutrients, healing medication and love to the development of a couple. In addition, communication eliminates poisons, wastes and hurt so that a couple can live healthily. Without communication, a couple would fall into silence, and their relationship would wither away and die. More importantly, conversation fulfills one of our most important emotional needs: the need to know and be known. *Please talk: I want to know you. Please listen: I want you to know me.* Communication is more than sharing information; it is the way people reach out and touch each other the most. Therefore, communication is very much a human, symbolic connecting, a social affair through which we share ourselves with others. Intimate communication is, at its core, the intent to love.

Communication is also the mediation of differences. Often it may seem that, in communication styles, men are from one planet while women are from another world entirely, speaking such different languages that understanding can be elusive and respect hard to grasp. Men may want results and communicate a "Mr. Fix-it" approach, while women seek more connection and respect, and desire to be listened to. Most of us are not well trained to listen.

Communication is, at the same time, a learned behaviour, a basic life skill and an art form. Communication is learned; it has a family-of-origin history, and we have had years of practice communicating the way we learned within our family of origin, for better or for worse. We each have our communication styles and idiosyncracies; we are convinced we know what we are doing and that we know how to communicate. Too often we think that communication comes naturally – after all, we have been doing it since the day we were born. But it is probably one of the main reasons cited for couple breakdown and a premier area of concentration and skills practised in therapy. There are ways to implement and master the steps of the dance of good communication.

When we begin to know ourselves better, we can also start to communicate that knowledge with our partner. As the communication channels open up, we learn even more about ourselves. It feels so good to be understood. Communication is that ritual (from the Latin word *ritus*, meaning "flow") that generates further discovery, information, patterns and connection. Effective communication makes the world go round and makes life work. Practising a new process of communication begins with knowing ourselves more and desiring to understand and appreciate our partner.

Each of us has the ability to change. We have to move from the old family rules, beliefs, stances of communication, ways of resolving differences and conflicts to a restructuring of our communication patterns. Old ways of communication need to be questioned and old habits often die hard. We need to create a new communication context and style to experience new ways of interacting, to reach a new understanding of how to become more human and fully alive. This is especially true for couple conflict. Communication reconstruction involves several steps. Through a re-enactment of the relationship patterns of our past, especially family-of-origin stories and patterns, we can acquire a better understanding of our struggles and yearnings. Then we need to construct how we want to be today, developing a new congruence with our present life yearnings.

Talk Nice! Listen Well! Don't Be Scared!

Couple relationships last mainly because of the partners' ability to resolve any disagreements that are an inevitable part of all relationships. I believe that three simple rules make up the core theory of good communication in couple relationships so that love can grow and partners can thrive: 1) talk nice, 2) listen well, and 3) don't be scared. More than just communication skills, talking nicely and listening well are characterized by our intention to be with our partner fully, to attend to him or her. As such, these are an act of love. As discussed in Chapter I, two family systems principles of adult maturity guide my communication theory: individuation and intimacy. *Individuation* is the process where one partner willingly and freely tells the other who they are, what they assume, feel, think, fear, want, etc. *"I want to be myself with you, and because I care enough, I will share myself with you."* We need to express our feelings, opinions and needs so that our partner can know who we are and what we want from them. Talking nicely is a form of self-disclosure that involves honesty, assertiveness, congruency and love. The couple relationship is a place where partners can feel free and safe enough to be themselves and to have the confidence to be able to say everything they believe and think. Although not all couples are in this place, they should be moving in this direction. If one partner is afraid of self-expression, for fear of being judged or silenced or rejected, then the couple still has quite a way to go. At the heart of the relationship must be the quality of listening, a listening that tenderly respects everything about the other. To achieve this, partners need to talk nicely to each other.

Speaking to your partner does not mean simply venting all our frustrations and anger, or criticizing, although there are times that frustration, anger and criticism need to be expressed. Above all, communication is about sharing our deeper feelings and motivations, hopes and expectations, wants and dislikes, and all that we want out of this relationship: *Where do I belong? To whom am I attached? Does he or she really know me?* Dialogue is a way of using ourselves as a gift to nurture and help our partner grow. Partners often grow very familiar with each other, but do not really know each other. They can assume a lot without checking it out: *"I could sense that she was a bit unhappy, but I never knew she was at the point of having an affair!"*

Couple development needs to consider the characteristics of each partner, their strengths and limitations, values, communication styles, and especially their family-of-origin wounds. It needs to focus on the history of the relationship and the patterns of interaction. It considers the thoughts, feelings and attitudes that energize in both a positive and negative manner. To know your own communication style better, you might want to try an experiment. Take your partner home for an evening with your family of origin. As you talk with your parents, your partner can objectively observe the communication patterns and give you feedback on how communication happened or did not happen.

Intimacy and connectedness is the principle that speaks of wanting to stay connected with our partner, even during a disagreement, and to appreciate that he or she is important to us. This is the art of listening well. Listening means that we appreciate our partner for many reasons, and want to understand them better. We want our relationship to work, to improve and to be life-giving for us. **Because we want to know our partner better, we want to listen well to all that is being communicated, to receive these messages, to ponder them.** It is said that it is often easier for couples to touch than to talk. Falling in love makes it clear that we can touch. Loving will determine if we can talk and share our inner selves.

In the Book of Genesis, one meaning of the word "to know" means to have intercourse with and to make love to, as in "Adam knew Eve" (Genesis 4:1). In other words, to know someone is the deepest expression of intimacy and connectedness that we human beings have. When the scriptures say that God knows us, the intent is to express a most intimate knowledge, to the point that God knows "all" about us — our gifts and our wounds — and still loves us. **Indeed, one definition of love can be "to know you and to be known by you."**

I believe that love wants to know and be known. When we first fall in love, we talk endlessly into the night so that our partner can know all about us. Probably the nicest thing about my marriage to my wife, Elizabeth, is that she knows me. At the same time, the most disconcerting thing about my relationship with Elizabeth is that she knows me! She knows my best side and my worst side, my strengths and my wounds.

Remember the old commercial where an elderly couple sits on the front porch, he on the bench and she in her rocking chair? At exactly the same moment, he moves his cup towards her and she reaches for the teapot and pours tea into his cup. They both do this without looking at each other — they know each other so well they can anticipate the other's move. It took a lot of talking and practice for this couple to get to know each other this well.

The Fear Factor

Fear is the greatest stumbling block to both love and communication. This fear might stem from a wound of childhood and often has one of two expressions: fear of intimacy or connecting, and fear of individuating or asserting oneself. According to the four attachment patterns described in Chapter 1, insecurity usually comes out of fear. Martin Luther King Jr. reminds us that people fear each other because they do not know each other. Fear of intimacy is that old feeling of being afraid to tell you who I am lest you might not like me, or being afraid to get too close lest you reject me, or being afraid to hear what you have to say to me. John Powell's book *Why Am I Afraid to Tell You Who I Am?* is still one of the greatest books in this area of communication. Powell's answer is striking: "I am afraid to tell you who I am, because, if I tell you who I am, you may not like who I am, and it's all that I have" (p. 12). Powell goes on to assert that we need to be free and willing to share our thoughts, values, fears, frustrations, greatness and failures with others. We need to tell them who we are (individuation) and that we want them to know us (intimacy).

Fear of individuating is the fear of asserting ourselves and standing up for our thoughts and feelings. Yet, partners need to put all sorts of issues and questions on the table of their relationship and be as honest as they can be, for there is much to gain in an open and frank discussion. Failure to do this can lead to a whole array of assumptions, and when we assume, we make an "ass" out of "u" and "me." Fear not! Good communication begins when we talk nicely and let our partner know who we are, listen well to appreciate them for who they are, and face the fears that might menace us and hold us back.

Communication 101

The process of basic communication involves both talking and listening in an intentional dance that requires both partners to be fully involved and enables both partners to reveal themselves. In communication, both the sender and receiver, the *talker* and the *listener*, have work to do. **The first task for you as the talker is to prepare what you want to say to your partner. It is important to collect your thoughts before speaking.** In addition to thinking things over in your head before you talk, you may want to write some feelings and thoughts on paper so that you are prepared to communicate the whole message. Preparing your words can also prevent self-criticism, such as "I wish I hadn't said that"; "I didn't really say what I meant to"; "I was so angry, I said all the wrong things." A lot of couples I see in couple therapy e-mail each other, or send handwritten letters as one means to communicate important issues. This is a particularly personal touch for many couples. Taking the time to write your message, rereading it and reflecting upon what you really want to say, and giving your message a "sober second thought" an hour later before pressing the send button are all helpful ways to communicate what you want to express. E-mails and letters also allow the listener or reader to ponder and reflect on what the message is saying and to have time to prepare a response.

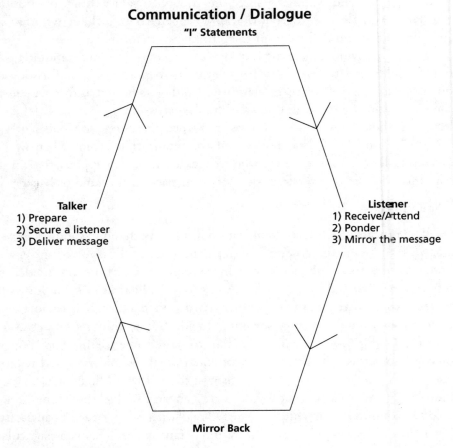

Communication / Dialogue
"I" Statements

Talker
1) Prepare
2) Secure a listener
3) Deliver message

Listener
1) Receive/Attend
2) Ponder
3) Mirror the message

Mirror Back

Love is "I am listening" / "I hear You."
I need to hear you, and I do not need to agree with what you say.

The second task of the talker is to be sure that you have a listener. Although it might sound silly, it is vital that your partner be ready and willing to listen before you begin to talk. If you sense that your partner is not listening, is distracted or is otherwise engaged, for heaven's sake, stop talking! You are not only wasting your breath but probably getting frustrated in the process. You might need to negotiate a good time to talk, and check with your partner to make sure he or she is ready to listen. Be creative! Invite your partner to dinner; set a positive tone in a relaxed, neutral atmosphere. The effort helps to set the stage for good communication, which your partner will appreciate.

The final task of the talker is to communicate the message. This message – of love, expectations, opinions, feelings, assumptions, issues, problems, wounds or observations – tells your partner what you need. Communication needs to be as "nice" and as honest as possible, without raised voices or condemnations. The Dialogue Wheel, which is presented a little later in this chapter, can be a good tool for constructive communication.

While one partner is speaking, the listening partner also has several tasks to do. **The first task for you as the listener is to attend to your partner and to your partner's words, trying to listen with empathy and interest.** Listening is one of the more important communication skills in the development of intimacy. One definition of love can simply be "I'm listening." Listening is a commitment and a compliment, and it is hard work. Listening says that we care enough about our partner to put aside our own needs of the moment, and we desire to hear, understand and know our partner better. Active listening is to attend to our partner as only a lover can do. While talking and listening are described above as two different tasks in communication, they happen simultaneously; we are always sending and receiving messages. Certainly one person needs to be the predominant sender and the other primarily a receiver, but in reality, each partner does both.

There are many blocks or types of communication "noise" that disrupt good listening. Some of these communication busters include habits such as mind reading, advising, fixing, judging or rehearsing your answer. All these are signs of defensiveness. Become aware of your reactive feelings while listening, but do not let your feelings overpower you: you will want to bring as much thoughtfulness as possible to bear in the listening process. Avoid interrupting or commenting; especially avoid facial expressions such as eye rolling or head shaking until the speaker is finished. Pause for ten seconds so you can ponder the message. This will allow you time to collect your thoughts and feelings about what is being said. The message can then sink in, and gives the speaker a sense of the importance of their message. When the message has been received, heard and pondered, repeat or mirror the basic message back to the speaker in such a way that the speaker is able to respond, "Yes, that is what I said. Thank you for listening."

Mirroring back to the speaker does not mean simply saying: "I heard you!" This is not good enough. The speaker needs to insist that the listener put the message in their own words. It is vital that the speaker and listener are working with the same message and are on the same page of understanding. Another "no-no" in communication happens when the listener becomes defensive and responds with a global statement, such as "Well, I hear that you don't love me!" when the speaker brings an irritating habit to the listener's attention. To mirror back is to reflect accurately the speaker's message, to the point where the speaker is satisfied that she or he has been heard. Hearing the message does not mean you have to agree with it, and the subject can be a matter for future communication. For the here and now, partners have a task — nay, a duty — to hear and acknowledge the message completely, even if they do not like or agree with it. This hearing of the message makes the communication circle complete. Thus, the process of communication is first, message spoken; second, message heard; and third, listening acknowledged.

If we could draw a map tracing the path or route that words of a message take, especially in enmeshed communication, it might look something like the following. Words are created in the speaker's gut or being, born in a fusion of feelings, observations, intuitions and old family-of-origin wounds. These words leave the speaker's mouth and enter the listener's ear. The words then drop quickly down to the listener's gut, where their old tapes or scripts are waiting and ready to interpret the words according to their wounds. These old wounds react automatically and instantaneously to the words heard and send out a reply through the listener's mouth back to the ears of the speaker, where, in the same manner, those words go to the speaker's wounded gut. So when partners are reactive or fighting, communication is the speaker's wound dancing with listener's wound, and most thoughtfulness has gone out the window. That slogan "Please engage brain before opening mouth!" is right on. Since the gut is faster than the brain and since emotional reactivity is quicker than thoughtfulness, we need to take the time and reflection necessary to communicate who we really are and how we want to be with our partner. We must also expect our partner to take the time and attention to hear our communication. As parents, we often tell our kids to take a time out because they are too emotional, yet few couples do the same for their conflictual confrontations.

Prayer for Couples

Divine Being,
Grant me the courage to tell my partner who I am,
The gentleness to listen well to who my partner is
And the wisdom to be true to both of us.

The Dialogue Wheel

The ability to communicate complete messages is an art well worth learning. One helpful tool is the Dialogue Wheel, adapted from *Love Knots*, by Lori Heyman Gordon (1990). The Dialogue Wheel is a structure that assists conversation, sharing, listening, getting to know each other. It is about getting to know ourselves and our partner. It can help our partner appreciate who we are, what we think, feel, want or do not want, and it can help us learn to appreciate our partner all over again. It is about connecting with our partner on a deep emotional level. The Dialogue Wheel helps couples to construct a new knowing and to narrate a new story that is us, like we did when we were first lovers. Dialogue raises a new awareness, a fresh appreciation and a novel thoughtfulness of ourselves and our partner and the way we dance our dance of intimacy together.

The Dialogue Wheel is meant as an aid to provide structure for non-threatening conversations. Because we are sometimes only vaguely mindful of what may be bothering us, the Dialogue Wheel provides starter sentences that are organized to help partners discover and sort out their perceptions, thoughts and feelings. The idea is to share information, feelings and opinions, and to see what meaning that might have for our partner. The purpose is to know the other better and be known by our partner. The Dialogue Wheel will also guide you in being specific about issues that might, at first sight, seem more vague. I have placed this Dialogue Wheel on the back of all my business cards and give it out freely to clients.

Dialogue Wheel

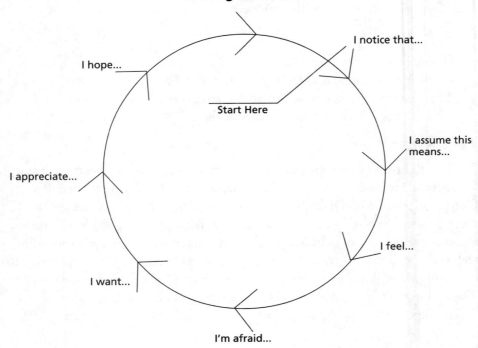

Notice that each statement begins with "I." Talk about yourself and share your own observations, assumptions, feelings, fears, wants. This is the stance of individuation and knowing yourself. You take responsibility for where you are, what you see or assume is going on between you. In a real sense, in the first moments, it is your own problem, and it might well become your problem as a couple as you continue to communicate because it will probably involve you. You need to be big enough to go first. Beginning conversations with the "You" word too often will put your partner on the defensive; they feel attacked, when, in truth, it is about you and what you may be observing, assuming, feeling or wanting. "You" is one of those dirty words in couple communication.

The Dialogue Wheel evolves like this:

I NOTICE ... relate behaviours (explicitly) or words spoken that you wish to address.

I ASSUME ... be up front with what you assume this means for you. Assumptions are often the cause of many arguments and need to be put on the table. Assumptions might be right or wrong, but they need to be clarified before mutual understanding can happen.

I FEEL ... one word or a few feeling words.

I AM AFRAID ... based upon your past experience, and projecting the interaction pattern into the future, with a leaning to predicting the worst.

I WANT ... be explicit and ask for the small things that can make a real difference. Avoid generalizations or dream-like wishes.

I APPRECIATE ... your partner as person, and something in particular about him or her now, as you have this conversation, including about this very topic. In a sense, this is the opportunity to compliment your partner, to be intimate and stay connected. It is meant as an "I love you" statement.

I HOPE ... a conclusion statement.

Example I: Dirty Dishes

Old Communication

You always leave your dirty dishes in the sink and you expect me to be your servant and clean up after you. You make me so mad! Why don't you act like a grown-up?

Dialogue Wheel

I notice that you left dirty dishes in the sink again and I assume you want me to clean up after you. When you do this, I feel used and frustrated. I am afraid that these actions lead me to think of you more and more as a child who cannot clean up after themselves. I want each of us to clean up after ourselves. I appreciate that you have had a busy, full day: so have I. I hope we can reach some understanding on how to handle these irritants.

Example 2: Late for Supper

Old Communication

If I've told you once, I've told you a thousand times: don't come home late for supper without calling me. Look! The supper is ruined and I ate alone. Do you think this is a restaurant? You make me so angry!

Dialogue Wheel

I notice that you come home late for supper quite a bit and you are not phoning me to let me know. I assume you think I should be just sitting here waiting for you. I feel frustrated and alone. I am afraid that when you do this, I will feel more distant from you. I want you to know that I will now only cook supper for myself unless you phone me to say you will be home for supper. I appreciate your busy schedule, and I hope you and I together can find ways to rectify this situation that will be acceptable to both of us.

I was doing family counselling with two parents and their two teenage daughters. I had introduced the Dialogue Wheel as one method to talk with each other. In the next session, the mother reported that one of the teenage girls had come to her during the week, holding the Dialogue Wheel card in her hand and saying, "I want to talk with you, Mom."

The Ten and Ten

Out of marriage encounter programs comes an old idea called the "10/10." It refers to a technique of communication where the couple sets aside twenty minutes several times a week just to talk to each other over any and all issues. The 10/10 is first and foremost a time just to talk and share and get to know the other again; it is also a time to connect in order to talk out issues and problems. Each partner has ten minutes to talk about whatever issue(s) he or she wants, at whatever speed they feel is comfortable, while the other partner listens. The listening partner is not allowed to interrupt or ask questions. As there may be times of silence within the ten minutes, playing some soft music can be a good idea. If the talking partner is using the Dialogue Wheel, the listening partner needs to allow them to go on right through the Dialogue Wheel until finished. The listening partner might even want to take a few notes during their ten minutes of listening, as a lot can be said, in order not to miss any of it. When ten minutes are up for one partner, the listening partner has ten minutes to talk about whatever she or he wants, either responding to the comments of the first ten minutes or moving on to another topic.

Many North American Native people use the sacred eagle feather in the ritual of communal communication. The eagle feather is farseeing and a symbol of all truth. Only one person can hold the sacred feather, and whoever holds the feather can speak their truth without interruption. When holding the eagle feather, all, including the Creator, take notice, and the holder of the feather is acknowledged with gratitude, love and respect. Communication may take a little longer, but when everyone is heard, decisions are usually wiser.

Finding a time to do the 10/10 — a quiet time, away from kids and disturbances — is a good beginning point. Going to a restaurant is a fine place to practise, for in restaurants, no one can scream or walk away. In the 10/10, present one issue at a time and stay with that issue until both partners are ready to let it go, or postpone it until another date. You can use a whole 10/10 for one issue. Using the Dialogue Wheel helps each partner stay on track and enables each to cover most aspects of an issue, such as particular behaviours or words, assumptions, feelings, fears, wants and hopes. It also adds the ingredient of appreciation for your partner.

The 10/10 enables the quiet partner to have space and to speak up, for he or she has ten minutes all to themselves. Quiet partners need the safety of knowing that they can speak at whatever speed they wish, and have time for silence. It allows them to prepare their thoughts and perhaps summon their courage. They are present simply by being there, and are speaking hopes and desires even if few words are spoken. The 10/10 enhances the power of communication in a couple by giving both partners equal time and opportunity.

Helpers and Pitfalls for Good Listening

True listening is a challenge that often fails, as the following poem tells us:

When I ask you to listen to me and you start giving me advice
   you have not done what I asked.
When I ask you to listen to me and you begin to tell me why
   I shouldn't feel that way, you are trampling on my feelings.
When I ask you to listen to me and you feel you have to do
   something to solve my problems, you have failed me, strange as that
   may seem.
So please, just listen and hear me. And if you want to talk,
   wait a few minutes for your turn, and I promise I'll listen to you.
—*Anonymous*

Many of us resist good communication. **The first communication pitfall is forcing the other to agree with your way of thinking.** Negotiating is part of couple relationships, and the goal needs to be a win-win situation where both partners feel comfortable. For one to be right, and to force the other to be wrong, will only lead to hurt feelings and distance and, in the end, both partners lose. **The second pitfall to communication is dwelling on mistakes, past and present.** A constant critical attitude undermines confidence and creates a negative flavour in the relationship. **The third pitfall of communication is using the conversation to punish your partner with insults and putdowns to win points at your partner's expense.** One example is the partner whose common phrase to his wife is to "be reasonable" — and then he goes on to express his way of what needs to be done.

The helpers of good communication are not strangers to partners, for they were almost effortlessly present in the days of being in love. In those days, kindness, consideration and interest were shared. Investing in these conversational skills helps couples maintain intimacy within their relationship. One helper of good communication is the old song "Getting to Know You, Getting to Know All About You" — using conversation to investigate, inform and understand each other. Interest in the other person is one of the main driving forces that leads to falling in love, and understanding helps relationships last. A second helper of good communication is developing an interest in each other's favourite topic of conversation. As relationships change and people grow, asking about your partner's day and particular area of interest is one sign of love that will always be appreciated. A third helper of good communication is balancing the conversation so that both partners feel heard and understood and appreciated. The key to good communication is giving each other your undivided attention. This may well mean setting aside time for each other, such as a walk or supper out just to enjoy each other and to talk. **"I am listening" is one of the better definitions of love.**

In couple communication and discussion, many partners think it is fine to end up with a win-lose situation; they think communication is some sort of debate where one opinion needs to carry the day and win at the other person's expense. In fact, there is no such thing as win-lose, for all win-lose endings really have a lose-lose ending. The losing partner often feels unheard, neglected, diminished or pushed aside, and this "losing" feeling will, in turn, often sabotage the "win" feeling of the other. Couple communication needs to strive for and accept nothing less than a win-win outcome so that both partners feel part of and significant in the dialogue. The win-win feeling enhances and strengthens a couple's relationship and love.

Verbal and Non-verbal Communication

Albert Mehrabian (1981) has found that communication is 7 per cent verbal (words), 38 per cent vocal (volume, tone, rhythm) and 55 per cent body movement. Thus, what speaks the loudest and most distinctly is the non-verbal body language used to express the message. The way we say things, more so than the words we use, emphasizes and reflects the feelings and emotional content of our communication. Facial expressions, vocal intonations, postures and gestures express the core message. When our non-verbal language contradicts the spoken message, people often see the incongruence and begin to mistrust the words themselves. The key here is congruence; the words, tones and body language must convey the same message.

Communication can be broken down into three parts: the explicit communication, the implicit communication and the null communication. Explicit communication is what is purposely and consciously being communicated. It is a combination of verbal and non-verbal communication; these need to be congruent so the talker and listener are on the same page of the dialogue. Implicit communication is an add-on to the explicit, and often deals with the communication of feelings, wants/needs or attitudes; in other words, it is more about emotions. This is the level of communication that often gets muddled and misunderstood, leaving partners wondering what is really being said. At this level, feelings such as love and dislike are often communicated. Null communication refers to all that is not being said, and may be conspicuous by its absence. There are times when saying nothing speaks volumes. When a couple has very little to say to each other in the evening, this may be one sign that the honeymoon is over, and old communication and intimacy wounds are dancing between them.

Example: Phil's Story

Phil grew up in a family where Mom was domineering, assertive and loud. "She ruled the roost," he would declare. When his wife communicated with similar aggressiveness and volume, Phil would quickly lose his temper, and the fight was on. When he began to observe and examine the communication components carefully, Phil realized it was all about tone, and how his wife's tone so resembled his mother's that it activated his old wound of feeling bossed, bullied and unable to get his own message across. Phil began to name that tone when he heard it, which allowed him to stay in the dialogue longer. His wife became more aware of her tone and was able to communicate in a different way.

From "You" to "I"

As we said earlier, the deadliest word in the communication of couples is probably the word "you" – as in "The trouble with you is..." or "You are the one who started this!" or "You think you're so perfect!" Once the finger is pointed at another, that person usually shuts down, the defensive walls go up and real communication stops. "You" is the word of blame, shame and guilt, and even though there are times when partners honestly need to wear one of these faults, there is a much better way of communicating the message: with the word "I." Notice that all the opening lines of the Dialogue Wheel begin with the word "I": I notice; I assume; I feel; I am afraid that; I want; I appreciate; I hope. Using I-statements enables people to take responsibility for their own thoughts and feelings and to initiate an open process of communicating with their partner. One of the better ways to move in the direction of good communication, to help your partner become more open and listening, is to open and reveal yourself to them – in other words, to be big enough to go first. Compare these two communications between partners.

Example I: Emotional Disconnection

#I: It is all your fault. The trouble with you is that you never take any initiative in trying to connect emotionally with me. I wait for you to talk to me, or invite me out for dinner, but no, sir! You make me so angry. Why don't you smarten up!

#2: I have noticed that we don't go out very much anymore, and I would really like to do that. Why don't you ask me out on a supper date, and we can talk about stuff? I would really like to spend some more time with you.

Example 2: Emotional Disconnection

#I. You drive me crazy! You have stopped listening to me, and now all you do is walk away. Why don't you tell me what you are thinking and feeling sometimes? Do you think I can read your mind?

#2. I have been feeling alone and ignored for some time now. It seems so hard for us to talk. I really want to know what you are thinking so that I can feel closer to you. Can we go out for dinner soon just to have some fun?

From "But" to "And"

Often couples who come into therapy use either/or statements, such as "Either you try to give me what I asked for or you don't really love me" or "If you loved me, you would want to touch me right now, but since you are not touching me, you obviously do not love me." These either/or statements paint partners into a corner: it has to be one or the other. Adults need to be able to hold on to more than one issue at a time.

Notice the difference between these two sentences:

I) I love you, BUT you make me so angry!

2) I love you AND, right now, I am feeling angry with what you did.

The "I love you" that was said before the "but" gets instantly forgotten and washed down the same drain of hurtful memory as the anger in the second part of the sentence. "But" calls out the defensive stances and places earplugs on the communication process. With "but," the second statement wipes out the first. On the other hand, partners can note that "and" moves the communication along smoothly and accurately while allowing more openness to happen. We are all mature enough to hold "I love you" and "I am angry" together, side by side, at the same time. Both are accurate reflections of the feelings that need to be expressed. "And" allows room for dialogue and compromise, and keeps partners connected while they deal with other interrelationship issues that need to be addressed. It maintains a safe, loving-enough environment while compromises are being sought.

From "Always/Never" to "Here and Now"

Another prevailing dialogue downfall is those sentences that contain the words "always" and "never." "You always do that!" or "You never give me what I need!" The use of these words, these emotional truths, leaves little or no room for manoeuvering and makes sure conversations stay stuck in the old places, unchanging. There is no longer any capacity to revisit the story, to reknow the other person, to revalue and appreciate aspects of the other. When we hold on to these words tenaciously, there is no room for other points of view. I have come to believe that "always" is "never" right and that "never" is "always" wrong. These words can readily be replaced with "often," or "rarely," or "from time to time": anything that allows room for movement in couple communication.

Communication is often called the work engine of a good marriage. In a healthy intimate relationship, communication needs to be working effectively, with both partners able to talk nicely, talk honestly, and listen appreciatively. Good conversation follows these steps:

1) planning time to talk: I need to talk with you; when is a good time?

2) talking nicely in I-statements, such as I notice – I feel – I want – I appreciate – I hope.

3) listening well, with undivided attention, by first of all mirroring or reflecting back what you have heard, stating that you can appreciate/

understand your partner for having said it, even if you do not agree with the statement. Develop an interest in your partner's favourite topic of conversation. If M. Scott Peck is correct in suggesting that marriage is a lot of work, then it is important to know that specific tasks and activities can enhance, enrich and move a good marriage into the realm of the "better."

Risks

To laugh is to risk appearing the fool.

To weep is to risk appearing sentimental.

To reach out for another is to risk involvement.

To expose my feelings is to risk exposing my true self.

To place my ideas and my dreams before another is to risk their loss.

To love is to risk not being loved in return.

To live is to risk dying.

To hope is to risk despair.

To try is to risk failure.

But risks must be taken, because the greatest danger is to risk nothing.

People who risk nothing, do nothing, have nothing and are nothing.

They learn to avoid suffering and sorrow,
but they cannot learn, feel, change, grow, love, live.

Chained by their certitudes, they are slaves and have forfeited their freedom.

Only the person who risks is free.

—*Anonymous*

Exercise I: Communication

The purpose of this exercise is to begin practising better communication by noting helps and blocks to good couple communication — things both of you would like to see changed so that communication can flow more freely.

To make our communication work for us, I think we need to try to

Stop Doing	Start Doing
1)	
2)	
3)	

To help our communication work for us, I want you to try to

Stop Doing	Start Doing
1)	
2)	
3)	

Exercise 2: Communication

The Communication Skills Test

Use this scale for the following questions:

Almost Never	Rarely	Sometimes	Quite Often	Most of the Time
1	2	3	4	5

1. People don't get what I am saying.   1 2 3 4 5

2. I pretend to listen even if my mind drifts away.   1 2 3 4 5

3. I find it hard to express my feelings.   1 2 3 4 5

4. I am afraid to tell people what I really want.   1 2 3 4 5

5. I tend to jump to conclusions.   1 2 3 4 5

6. I become defensive when I feel criticized.   1 2 3 4 5

7. I tend to lose control of my emotions
when trying to resolve difficult problems.   1 2 3 4 5

8. I tend to postpone discussing touchy topics.   1 2 3 4 5

9. I would rather talk about you than talk about me.   1 2 3 4 5

10. I am scared to tell you the whole story because
you might like me less.   1 2 3 4 5

Scoring

10-20 Very good communication skills

21-30 Good communication skills

31-40 Poor communication skills

41-50 Very poor communication skills

8
Re-creating the Relationship III:
Emotional Connectedness

All the knowledge I possess everyone else can acquire,
but my heart is all my own.
　　—Johann Wolfgang von Goethe (1749–1832)

Love is our true destiny. We do not find the meaning of life by ourselves
alone – we find it with another. We will never be fully real until we let
ourselves fall in love – either with another human being or with God.
　　—Thomas Merton, Love and Living

There can be no knowledge without emotion.
We may be aware of a truth, yet until we have felt its force,
it is not ours. To the cognition of the brain
must be added the experience of the soul.
　　—Arnold Bennett (1867–1931)

Ways of Connecting

Lerner (1989) describes intimacy as the ability to be yourself in a relationship and to allow your partner to do the same. Being yourself means knowing who you are (Know Thyself, Chapter 6) and choosing to communicate who you are to your partner openly and clearly (Communication, Chapter 7). To "allow your partner to do the same" means staying connected emotionally, in a way and in a place that is safe and trusting for both partners. **Emotional connectedness is the ability to balance individuation and intimacy /**

togetherness in such a way that we can both live and love with a good understanding and appreciation of who we are. We need to do this loving in a space that is secure for both partners.

The pivotal access to change and growth for couples is found in the awareness of their underlying emotions. Each of us encompasses emotional components that form primary needs within our being. Some deeply experienced emotions such as security, trust, love, connectedness and freedom are vital for couple life, as these lead to a positive and enriching loving spiral within the couple. Harmonious couple relationships are, in their essence, emotional connections in a safe and trusting meeting place. The vast majority of ways to create trusting emotional connections are born, learned and developed within our family of origin, and they are a part of our personality by the time we are six to ten years old. We probably have learned and have been practising both positive and negative emotional connections constantly throughout our lives, and these ways of connecting are already an intimate part of our relationship style when we meet our new partner.

It Takes Two to Tango

Maintaining contact with a significant other is a primary motivating principle for all human beings. Feeling secure with another person is a basic need for all people, for love enhances confidence and sharing. Couple relationships wax and wane over the years, as both partners work on the delicate balance of individuation and intimacy, of attachment and autonomy. It takes two to make love and two to fight; I believe that, for the most part, we dance this dance of intimacy, and its corresponding dance of wounds, in equal portions. It takes two to tango at this depth of relationship. Both partners push and pull, step forward and back, give and receive love. Both partners are responsible for knowing themselves and take ownership for their contribution to the loving and to the conflict. Finger pointing does very little good here, while I-statements are a blessing.

When couple relationships get stuck and negative spirals seems to be the rule for the relationship, the challenge to change the steps of the dance is an urgent one. Partners have choices here: they can either put all or most of the blame on the other ("It's all your fault") or they can look more closely at both themselves and their partner and realize that "we" have a problem; "we" are caught in the dance of wounds and "we" need and want to find a way out for us. To untangle the dance of wounds, one person needs to start by saying, "I want to make our relationship better; here are a few things that will need to change." (See the exercise at end of this chapter.) When both partners admit fault and seek repair and greater emotional connectedness, the dance of wounds can become a tango of love again.

Negative and Positive Interactional Cycles and Spirals

When the dance of wounds is fully operative, couples are caught in negative interactional cycles such as criticize and withdraw, over-responsible and under-responsible, pursue and flee. The common dynamic for this dance of wounds is often too much intensity by one partner and too much distance by the other. Too much intensity is that preoccupied/enmeshment pattern when one partner is overly focused on what their partner is or isn't doing and attempts to blame the other and demand that they change. Too much distance is avoidant/cut-off and often means that there is insufficient sharing and talking in the relationship and togetherness has been minimalized. Couples can get stuck in these negative interactional cycles and the dance of wounds rules the day. These interactional positions in distressed couples tend to become rigidly defined, creating powerful negative feedback cycles. Partners react to each other with strong emotional states, such as fear, anger, depression, distance or enmeshment. These patterns can take on a life of their own and become self-reinforcing, restricting emotional accessibility and responsiveness, which are the basis of a secure sense of attachment and connectedness. **Inasmuch as this dance of wounds looks like distrust and alienation, it may also be seen as a strong desire to recapture the love and connection that used to be present within the couple relationship when the two people originally fell in love.**

It's hard to say who begins a negative spiral. Sure, people are very willing to point the finger and blame their partner with lines like, "You started it when you...," but the truth is not that clear, for both partners often use a long litany of defences, such as, "Yes, but first you did. . . ." Often couples stay stuck at this level of blaming the other, which is like a "hole in the sidewalk" that neither can get out of on their own.

Unlike negative spirals, which happen more or less automatically as a result of the dance of wounds, positive spirals need to be built, block by thoughtful block, step by conscious step, stage by loving stage. There must be a willingness to want to work on positive spirals. Wounds, especially love and relationship wounds, which are the results of deficits of love in childhood, can only be healed through the gentle love of a partner, a friend, a parent, a therapist, a child or, for many, God. **The first step in the dance of re-creating the relationship requires an intimate, continuous, reliable and predictable relationship with another; we can then feel secure and loved enough to open up and talk about our wounds so that healing can now begin.** The healing of wounds, in this sense, involves the recognition of our wounds (Chapter 6), their beginnings in our family of origin (Chapter 1), communication of wounds with our significant other (Chapter 7) and feeling safe and being touched by appropriate love (Chapter 8). In other words, the childhood wound of a deficit of love is allowed to surface and is responded to with gentle and persistent affection. This new, positive dance opens up space and a new dialogue that creates new steps in the positive spiral of the couple's dance. Positive steps in the relationship establish a more secure base, which in turn generates a more positive attachment between the partners, and love can be rebuilt. Couples begin to validate each other's experience and to communicate more openly. To come to the point in the development of a couple relationship where partners can open up to each other in a secure place and ask the other's help with their wound is one of the great definitions of love.

Big Enough to Go First

So, who goes first? On the outside of a card a friend sent me are these words: "Let us share the deepest, darkest secrets of our souls." Inside the card it reads, "You go first!" **When the red flags fly in couple interactions and everyone knows that something is wrong in the relationship, who will be the first to say, "Stop! Time out! We have a problem here! My buttons are being pushed and I am hurting. My wounds are starting to dance! We need to do something different"?** Love means committing ourselves to healing the couple relationship and to risk giving ourselves, without a guarantee of return, in the hope that our work and our love will produce healing. Going first is a real act of faith.

How often I hear the same tune in therapy, when one partner knew for years that there was something wrong, but never said anything, or did so in feeble utterances. "I just thought you stopped loving me and did not care anymore, so I went on my way." On the other end of the spectrum, some partners have an affair, which is one big, loud (albeit inappropriate) cry for help. As indicated in both scenarios, more often than not, partners do signal trouble in the relationship in some way, by anger or withdrawal, in quiet gestures or in loud scenes. It takes courage to signal our dissatisfaction within the couple relationship and even more courage to say it directly to our partner.

Once we have communicated to each other that the relationship is in trouble, it takes even more courage and thoughtfulness to begin to re-examine the relationship problems and determine a path of corrective action towards new emotional connectedness. Who is big enough to suggest couple help? Which partner has the courage to propose therapy? Can you begin the process of putting issues on the communication table and looking at the issues and wounds that spawned this dance of wounds in the first place? My experience has taught me that if a couple has drifted some distance apart and the issues are substantive, it is best to put all issues on the table of therapy and be honest in the work of couple reconstruction. Give it all you've got! When couple work needs to be done, to try — as in the statement "I am going to try" — is not enough. Either you do the work of loving or you don't. Either someone becomes big enough to go first or nothing changes. In other words,

Dance like no one is looking.
Love like you have never been hurt.
Give like you are a millionaire.
Talk like newfound lovers.
Have the courage to go first.

Focusing on Emotions

Becoming aware of our emotional reactions is the best route to shaping new responses. We need to focus on our deepest feelings and needs and express these to our partner.

Restructuring the dance of wounds happens when we reshape emotional responses. The dance of wounds, expressed in hurt, rejection and dismissal, needs to change into a dance of re-creating relationship by means of connection and togetherness. Re-creating the relationship requires the following steps:

- increased awareness of the present pain that both partners are feeling;
- acknowledgment of the hurts present in the dance of wounds and how both partners are contributing to the problem;
- helping partners connect with their own deeper selves, including pains and wants;
- talking and truly listening;
- curiosity leading to knowing, appreciating and understanding each other;
- creating a safe place to come together and talk.

There needs to be a softening: an honest, gentle sharing of wants, needs, opinions, feeling; an appreciation of our partner and all they are, say and feel; a safe place to meet, to talk and to touch. Emotions are of central importance in relationships, and can lead a couple to positive new insights in the re-creation of the relationship. Emotions are the glue that holds couples together. The dance of re-creating relationships happens when new experiences of relationship patterns are set up so that security is acknowledged, trust is met and both partners are open to engage in greater accessibility and responsiveness.

Example: John and Susan's Story

John and Susan had been feeling distant from each other for months. They had spoken some cruel words to each other, especially about the hurt both were feeling in regard to what each perceived they were not receiving from the other. During therapy, Susan seemed to be first to see her contribution to the couple problem and wanted to move in the direction of trying harder, including reconciliation. John was more reluctant, holding onto his hurt longer. He stated that the "feeling of being in love" was gone and he wanted to feel a sense of loving Susan again. John said to Susan: "When I long for you, I can reconnect with you." Gradually, through lots of walks and talks and lots of tears, this longing grew, but it was a different kind of love than the original "falling in love." Susan and John were moving towards a new and deeper connection at an emotional level.

Availability, Affection and Affirmation

What is this affective fuel that keeps a couple going? How is the emotional encounter sustained? Are there ways of connecting emotionally that build trust and safety in a couple relationship? There are five healthy methods of moment-to-moment loving: availability, demonstration of affection, affirmation, communication and resolution of conflict. We have covered the last two items in Chapter 6 (Communication). Let us turn now to the first three methods.

The first dimension of emotional connection is availability and a lived sense of being together, living in the same ballpark of intimacy. Couples nourish each other by their mutual company, going for walks together, sitting and talking, and going to bed together. Throughout these times, they watch and listen to each other, touch and smell. All this happens quite naturally and is not consciously registered until one partner goes away for a while, or the sense of togetherness is missed. Availability is made difficult in today's world when both partners work outside the home, the calendar gets full of "things to do" and the weekend is spent shopping. A regular dinner date, a weekend away together and conversations over coffee are the moments that help keep couples connected emotionally. This offers them a secure base through which their relationship can be gradually re-created.

With availability must also come demonstrations of affection: hugs, caresses, kisses and snuggles. During a therapy session, one woman said to her husband that what she really wanted from him was a big hug, a passionate kiss, a tête-à-tête and a compliment each day. This was, of course, the glue in the early years of the relationship when they could not wait to touch each other. Over time, perhaps with familiarity or perhaps with changes in the bio-chemical makeup of each partner, or perhaps with the arrival of kids and fatigue setting in, affection is decreased, and, at times, almost lost. Men are often not as good at, and may feel embarrassed by, demonstrations of affection other than sex. Women rejoice in touch and can feel neglected by its demise. Women enjoy affection separate from sex, while men find that difficult to fathom. The lived reality of sex in couple relationships, and the poor communication about the affection and sexual needs of each partner, is one of the common stumbling blocks of relationships and is often much in need of repair through therapy.

Sexual intercourse is a primary expression of love, and it is about a whole lot more than orgasm. Touch, smell, taste and words all speak to one another a language of love. Sex is also a very personal language of love, something held exclusively and privately within couple relationships. Sex conveys the message that we want, appreciate and know our partner. It is also a powerful affirmation of each other's identity as woman and man. Sex is often an expression of reconciliation and thanksgiving.

Affirmation is another method of loving. Complimenting and affirming each other is the oxygen of self-esteem. We all need it. Yet somehow when the relationship gets on in years, we neglect or forget to affirm. We tend to keep our mouths shut when things go well and open when things go wrong, especially when we feel wronged by our partner. Affirmation talks about appreciating, understanding, encouraging, approving. Gottman suggests that we accentuate the positive in our couple relationships while dealing with the negatives as they come up.

To Appreciate the Other as Other

Our partner is more than the person we first fell in love with. As we saw earlier in this book, each partner has family-of-origin and other wounds, including possible wounds around individuating and connecting, communicating, touching and sex, and a whole host of other values that make each of us unique. It is fairly easy to appreciate these qualities in our partner while we are in love; yet, as the honeymoon comes to a close and the dance of wounds begins, much of this previous appreciation seems to go out the window. Indeed, partners often begin to see each other as purposely withholding love or even as being downright mean. Learning to know and appreciate each other for who we are includes acknowledging and working with our partner's woundedness with the same sense of charity and acceptance as we expect them to have regarding our wounds. In other words, **our partner is both the loving, caring and exciting person that we first fell in love with AND a limited and hurting person with wounds, somewhat equal to our own.** We have chosen a partner of equal maturity and now both of us dance the dance of wounds in more or less equal contributions. So, when we need to know, to understand and to appreciate our partner, we need to accept all aspects of our partner, and begin our work of re-creating the relationship, especially by connecting emotionally. We need to see ourselves and our partner as both loving and wounded.

The process of change in couple therapy is a constant movement from conscious effort to more conscious effort until our emotional connectedness becomes more natural. This process of appreciating the other as other (loving *and* wounded) means taking time together and getting into the communication of issues. It speaks of creating that safe-enough place where hurts and wounds can be expressed and dealt with in an accepting fashion. This may mean becoming creative in loving and finding ways of keeping the romance alive in the relationship.

Share Your Hopes and Dreams

Dreams and hopes also have tremendous power. Dreams speak of the possibilities of the future. When shared and pursued, they have the power of making themselves come true, the power of self-prophecy. Dreams add a component of wonder and surprise that gives relationships direction and connectedness at a deeper, almost mystical emotional level. In the re-creating of your relationship, ask yourselves what you would want the relationship to look like in six to nine months. What qualities does each of you seek to have active in your relationship? What are you willing to do and change to attain these qualities? Sharing your hopes and dreams is the beginning of making the miracle come true.

Moving a Relationship from "Good" to "Better"

Most marriages begin with love and "good" intentions. People marry because they want to give the best to their partner, and hope for love/care/friendship/intimacy in return. And yet, this movement between "the happiest day of your life" and "living happily ever after" seems to elude most people. Approximately 40 per cent of marriages end in divorce. Peck boldly states that, after the falling in love part, a relationship is a lot of work.

We all have emotional needs, and it is an almost unspoken expectation that our partner should know and provide for our needs. After all, isn't that what love is all about? Well, yes and no. Yes, love wants to give the best to the other: and no, we need to be careful when we assume that our partner knows and is able to provide for all of our needs. Partners need to identify their own and their partner's emotional needs and learn to become experts in trying to meet these needs. Research has outlined the most important emotional needs. In the following exercise, you are encouraged to rank these needs for yourself and your partner. Then talk about your differences. Talking through each partner's ranking of emotional needs allows for the sharing of couple strengths, invites the soothing of hurting areas and acknowledges unspoken differences.

Emotional Needs	My Ranking	How My Partner Would Rank
To be loved		
To feel safe and secure		
Sexual fulfillment		
Communication		
Having fun together		
Honesty and openness		
An attractive partner		
Financial security		
Helping out around the house		
Commitment to the family		
To be appreciated		

"I've Learned"

1. I've learned that you cannot make someone love you. All you can do is be someone who can be loved. The rest is up to them.

2. I've learned that no matter how much I care, some people just don't care back.

3. I've learned that it takes years to build up trust and only seconds to destroy it.

4. I've learned that it is not what you have in life that counts, but who you have in life that counts.

5. I've learned that it takes me a long time to become the person I want to be.

6. I've learned that you should always leave loved ones with loving words. It may be the last time you see them.

7. I've learned that you can keep on going after you think you can't.

8. I've learned that we are responsible for what we do, no matter how we feel.

9. I've learned that either you control your attitude or it controls you.

10. I've learned that no matter how hot and steamy the relationship is at first, the passion fades and there had better be something else to take its place.

11. I've learned that sometimes when I am angry I have a right to be angry, but that doesn't give me the right to be cruel.

12. I've learned that true friendship continues to grow. Same goes for true love.

13. I've learned that because someone doesn't love you the way you want them to doesn't mean they don't love you with all they have.

14. I've learned that no matter how good a friend is, they're going to hurt you every once in a while, and you must forgive them for that.

15. I've learned that our background and circumstances may have influenced who we are, but we are responsible for who we become.

16. I've learned that two people can look at the exact same thing and see something totally different.

—*Anonymous*

Exercise: Emotional Connection

This exercise is designed to help couples name and claim those emotional connections that enhance trust and security in the relationship. These might include emotional connections from the early days of falling in love, or better still, new expressions of feeling connected today.

What I like best about you is:

1)

2)

3)

In terms of feeling emotionally connected, what I need most from you right now is:

1)

2)

3)

9

Re-creating the Relationship IV:
Spirituality and Forgiveness

I walk down another street.
> — *Portia Nelson, "Autobiography in Five Short Chapters"*

Lift up your eyes
and look on one another in innocence
born of complete forgiveness
of each other's illusions.
> —*A Course in Miracles*

Genuine forgiveness is participation,
reunion overcoming the powers of estrangement.
We cannot love unless we accept forgiveness,
and the deeper our experience of forgiveness is,
the greater is our love.
> —*Paul Tillich*

Couple Spirituality

If the primary dynamic of couple relationships is love, and if we believe that God is love, it would make great sense to find a meaningful place for spirituality in the development of your couple relationship. Spirituality is all about God with us in whatever specific terms we may choose to express our experience of God. It can be a spiritual experience for couples to share emotional and physical intimacy: to give birth to a child; to share honestly with each other; to care for frail parents, partners and children; to give and receive love and forgiveness. Worded another way, **couple spirituality is about being-in-relationship, whether that is being-in-relationship with our partner, family, children, others or nature, or Being-in-relationship with God.** Couple spirituality experiences both as aspects of one and the same relationship. Mary Anne McPherson Oliver suggests that couple spirituality moves from an individualistic concept and relationship with the Divine being and resolves to locate the centre of spiritual attention to the relationship itself and in those sacred spaces between the partners. In other words, where two gather, God is in their midst. Living life in touch with our spirituality lets us as a couple see the light of love in all aspects of our lives. In this sense, spirituality and love accent the basic connectedness of life. The Latin verb *con-jungere*, as in conjugal love and spirituality, means to bind together, to unite, to connect. Spirituality is a way of living and seeing love lived. This is a fundamental spirituality for couples and families.

Love is that force that all the great religions have seen as the supreme unifying principle of life. Saint John writes: "Let us love one another, for love is God and everyone that loves is born of God and knows God" (I John 4:7). Thus, the spirituality of Being-in-relationship is about how partners and love and God all mingle together in the journey called life. Couple and family relationships are at the heart of the practice of love. Thomas Merton says that we do not become fully human until we give ourselves to one another in love. In fact, the spiritual life of loving one other person, such as in a couple relationship, requires conscious practice and a willingness to bring all aspects of our lives into loving action. This spirituality of Being-in-relationship has many expressions. Love is about being vulnerable and accepting that each partner has gifts and wounds; love is about creating that balance between self and partner, between autonomy and connection; love is about creating meaningful memories and taking the time to savour these couple times; love is about actively waiting for our partner to attend to us emotionally and physically, to communicate with us; love is about recognizing growth in each other, accepting and forgiving when some things just cannot be changed. Being-in-relationship also demands commitment. The spirituality of Being-in-relationship calls couples to try to be as loving with each other as God is with us.

The Road to Emmaus

A beautiful gospel story, the Road to Emmaus (Luke 24:13-35), can serve as the backdrop for the place of Being-in-relationship in couple spirituality. I'll give it a slight translation for this couple audience.

Two people, a couple, are journeying along, "talking with each other about all the things that had happened." It seems that they had been living a beautiful experience together these past years, being-in-relationship with each other and Being-in-relationship with God. Their initiation into this relationship had been exciting and full of promise. During these years they knew life, generosity and the peace that came from love for each other, their families of origin and the larger community. They were committed to each other. But lately, part of their journey had become confused and they were feeling alienated and lost. They felt they were on the road, fleeing because of the doubt and disappointment that existed in their relationship with God and with each other. Their initial dream was being covered in darkness; their hope seemed to be vanishing; love seemed dead. They "stood still, looking sad."

Along comes a stranger, someone who wants to Be-in-relationship with them, and this Being asks them what their journey has been like. "What is this conversation that you are holding with each other as you walk?" As they tell their story of their life together, it becomes evident that this Being is not only listening, but is also deeply concerned and interested in them. "What things?" the Being asks, encouraging them to be exact and to talk about their deeper feelings. As they open themselves to the gentle empathy of this Being, the couple begins to see that the Being knows much more than they first thought. Through concern and curious questions, the Being gets the full story. "Was it not necessary that love should suffer these things?"

The Being begins to interpret for this couple possible meanings for their experiences of distance, placing these into the bigger picture of life and encouraging them both to reflect. "From the beginning, the Being interpreted to them all the things concerning love." The couple and this Being walk and talk all that day. Slowly things begin to stir in the couple's hearts, but they are too shy or blocked to say anything to each other. Their hearts seem ready, but they await the moment of grace.

That evening, when they stop to partake of the bread of their unity, "their eyes were opened and they recognized love and Being-in-relationship in their midst again." They discover a new and much deeper meaning together: life is renewed; Being-in-relationship is alive again within them. And they remember, "Did not our hearts burn within us as Being-in-relationship talked to us on the road and opened to us the meaning of love?" With life and love renewed, they immediately set out for home. The place that was once darkness and disillusionment could again be the place where love and life abound.

There are three stages of life in Eastern spiritual thought. The first stage, called learning, covers ages 0 to 20; the second, called family, spreads over ages 20 to 40; the third, called spirituality, goes from age 40 to the end of life. There is a strong sense of being in relationship in each these three stages. Spirituality is rooted in our family-of-origin learned experiences, and it grows in proportion to the ways our parents love us. Spirituality is handed down in the experiences of loving that we learn within our family of origin, that we live with our partner and hand down to our children. Often our spiritual beliefs are passed down from generation to generation without much thought or reflection. It may only be in the latter part of our lives that we engage in spirituality more as a life integration experience, yet this cannot readily be separated from earlier family-of-origin and love relationship experiences of life. The spirituality of Being-in-relationship is inherently relational and is expressed best in caring.

Spirituality may be one of the untapped springs of change and healing in the ongoing development of couple relationships. This spiritual awakening creates a powerful demand for individuals and couples to become more aware of, and sensitive to, religious and spiritual issues and a new way of being in relationship. It appears that marriage and family theory is only beginning to study the supporting role of spirituality in the growth process of couples and families. Articles on the delineation of a spirituality for couples, as well as spiritual development for both partners, are rare and are usually individually oriented or found in the fields of theology and religion. This chapter sets out a more universal spirituality for couple development presented in the framework of Being-in-relationship – a model that can lead to new areas of exploration for couples. After looking at the meaning of spirituality in general, we will explore several universal spiritual images as a spiritual growth model for couples in particular. These spiritual themes include vulnerability, to know and be known, the paradox of love, commitment and forgiveness.

Spirituality

The spirituality of Being-in-relationship is defined or described broadly. We'll look at three main aspects or definitions of spirituality here: 1) a spirituality lived through faith or attunement with God, gods, the Divine or soul; 2) a spirituality lived in hope and finding meaning, purpose and values in our lives; and 3) a spirituality expressed in love through connecting with other people, especially partners, on the journey of life. In short, couple spirituality is about being in relationship with God, being in relationship with life, and being in relationship with others, especially our partners, children and family of origin.

Spirituality is, for most people, first of all about attunement with God or the Divine, a dimension of human experience that includes awareness of the existence of a Divine Being, an innate yearning for connection with this Being, and a belief that this Being is interested in and acts in the relationship with us. This is the spirituality of Being-in-relationship. This faith in a transcendent Being carries with it an invitation to conform our lives to this higher power. God can provide the unifying force that brings stability, meaning and purpose to life. Spirituality is distinguished from religion or morality: spirituality is seen as a personal and subjective experience of the Divine Being, while religion refers more specifically to concrete expressions of spirituality (rituals, doctrines, practices). Spirituality also carries a greater sense of openness, curiosity and wonder, while religion tends to convey more certitude.

Spirituality also has to do with how people courageously attempt to sort out their awareness of reality so as to harvest a more satisfactory meaning of life. Spirituality may be defined as a fundamental meaning-making process in which human beings try to make sense of their awareness of life by finding a place for everything in their experience and by assigning everything to its perceived proportionate/appropriate place. This is a spirituality of being in relationship with life. It is about exercising values, either by seeking to apply a value system, or re-creating a value orientation as a way of making sense out of life. The theme of meaning-making is often linked to hope. Spirituality is, therefore, the capacity for engaging in a variety of ways of looking at life as well as making differential connections between experiences. This capacity includes transforming former, now unsatisfactory, ways of putting life together and focusing on opening up new, more inclusive ways of being in relationship with life's experiences.

Lastly, spirituality has a dimension of connecting with other people, what might be termed a spirituality of being in relationship with others. This is a process of being rooted and seems to have its genesis in the Latin root of the word "religion," *religare*, which can be taken to mean "to bind together" or "to make connection with." One aspect of this spirituality is where "two or more gather together, God is present as Being-in-relationship." It is an expression of spirituality described as affiliation or connection, and can be expressed as belonging to a particular faith tradition or group. This is especially true for couples who value a spiritual dimension to their life together. To know our partner is to allow them the freedom to participate in their own variation of spirituality. Couples do not necessarily have to believe the same creeds of faith, although there is some evidence to suggest that a commonness in the spiritual journey enriches the couple relationship. But we do have to know and respect our partner's spiritual journey, however different it might be from our own. Further, we need to appreciate and encourage each other's spiritual journey and practices, as these are integral expressions of ourselves. Talking about and sharing each other's spiritual experiences can strengthen the relationship.

Spirituality: Entering into Vulnerability

Most world religions would agree that there is only one royal road for the spiritual journey, and that is love. In fact, many spiritual writers would say there is but one religion, the religion of love. "This is my commandment, that you love one another," the gospel tells us (John 15:12). To love another, especially our partner, has many implications. It is more than talk or touch, more than fun or sex. Love speaks of knowing and being known, of giving to the other, of being vulnerable with the other, of forgiving the other, of being in relationship. All these are possible within our commitment to love.

The essential purpose of spirituality is to liberate us from clinging to a narrow, conditioned, self-defined perception established by our past, perhaps within our family-of-origin experiences, and to open us up to something much larger. Being at the centre of this opening up means entering into vulnerability and freeing ourselves from unredeemed wounds, such as clinging to the old attachment patterns or the fear of entering into new ways of being in relationship. This is especially true when it comes to opening ourselves in one of the most challenging areas of life: personal relationships, intimacy, sex, love and passion – in other words, couple relationships. It is often easier to enter the spiritual realm alone than with another person. Perhaps that is why spirituality has so long been the domain of monks, priests, nuns and hermits. In today's world, the need for a fully developed couple spirituality is all the more urgent. In couple relationships, our partner inevitably mirrors to us both our love and our wounds, and begins to tell us how these affect him or her. As a result, we must face our vulnerability in an open and expanded manner. In Buddhist spiritual terms, this requires a new awakening, a new way of thinking and loving, a new way of being in relationship with our partner. This may mean taking a new look within ourselves, to know ourselves and see ourselves as God sees us.

To attach to a partner after separating from our family of origin, to re-create a couple relationship or to reconnect with family after an estrangement requires an entry into vulnerability. This might be described as a new experience in the sociological womb, to give rebirth to who we are: to be born again and feel secure. How can couples create such a safe and trusting place within which each can become more open to the other? The task of lovers is not just to enjoy each other but to call each other to wholeness and re-creation. This courage to enter vulnerability is exercised when partners dare look at their own wounds and their own contribution to any couple problem (Chapters 1 and 6). Each couple discovers their own unique dance of wounds, often by trial and error, and thus their own version of couple spirituality and entry into vulnerability. It is also present when partners reconnect at a deeper emotional level (Chapter 8). Spirituality is about partners encouraging each other and allowing each other time and space to open up to greater and deeper meanings in life and in their relationship. Sharing spirituality is being in relationship and sharing intimacy at its deepest level.

Worded another way, if our spirituality helps us believe that God loved us first, that God is big enough to forgive us first, that God is open enough to know us first, that God is safe enough and a "good enough mother" for us to find security and trust in, if God is daring enough to do all this for us, then we might also find the courage to do the same for our partner. As God is love, so too partners are called into loving gestures. Being big enough to go first, being able to enter into vulnerability with our partner, is one sign of Being-in-relationship.

The story is told about the marriage therapist who is working with a couple. The therapist asks the couple about their financial issues, and the couple gladly shares both their resources and the issues that arise from this area of their relationship. The therapist then asks about their love and sex life, and again the couple is quick to share their joys and conflicts in this area of their relationship. Lastly, the therapist asks about their spirituality and how they live it. They turn to the therapist and say, "You're getting kind of personal, aren't you?"

Spirituality: To Know and Be Known

The longing to know and be known by another is powerful indeed. Authenticity and empathy are necessary couple values. **The best thing about marriage is that my partner knows me; the worst thing about marriage is that my partner knows me!** In the Christian scriptures, love is defined as "knowing." To enter into knowing our partner and to allow ourselves to be known by our partner can often feel like a long and vulnerable journey. Relationships have such hopeful and blissful beginnings as couples talk away the night in love and make love in an almost desperate need to get to know each other. Gradually, however, the honeymoon wanes and self-protective ego walls spring back up between partners. Soon, more and more personal aspects become clouded in unknowns and confusions and assumptions and hurts; the original family-of-origin wounds dance openly before both partners. It is like we do not know each other anymore. Dare I enter into vulnerability again, and open myself to let you know me, now with my wounds and all?

The Buddhist tradition includes a beautiful concept of friendship called *Kalyanamitra*, the noble friend. Your noble friend will not accept pretense and will gently and surely confront you with your own blindness. Each of us has blind spots and wounds, for no one can see life totally. I must depend upon another to see those parts and aspects of myself that I cannot see. In a sense, partners complement our vision, sometimes in a kind way, other times in a critical way. Such relationships are both creative and beneficial, and they may point out and negotiate both giftedness and wounds. Only in this way can we truly see and know ourselves. The honesty and clarity of such a true relationship bring out the real contour of our person. Spiritual practice, when divorced from the textures of personal life, can be dry and remote; life can remain narrow and confining when cut off from the fresh breezes of spiritual realization. So, too, love can become stagnant when challenges to growth and change are left untended. Perhaps the most vulnerable statement we can say to our partner is, "This is my wound: help me!"

One important source of spiritual growth is communication with like-minded people, especially our partner. When we open up to each other again in search of the healing of our family-of-origin wounds, when we search for a way of loving that honours our emotional connectedness, when we care enough and dare enough to go first in the exercise of knowing ourselves or communicating this to our beloved, then love is real and God is there in relationship with us. Put another way, when we live our spiritual life deeply and we know that God is there, then we have the strength to love and be with each other.

Example: Henri Nouwen's Story

After meeting the writer Henri Nouwen years ago and reading biographies of his life, I began to know something about his inner struggles, especially his family-of-origin wounds. I saw that it was as if he were working out these struggles though his writings. Amidst the great spiritual inspirations within his books, Henri seemed to struggle much with his own lovability, his sexuality and his loneliness. Indeed, Henri's struggle with his lovability is integral to his family-of-origin wounds and his spirituality: he described himself as the "wounded healer." Henri came from a wealthy background with a loving, warmhearted mother and a more distant, success-driven father. Michael Ford, in his portrait of Henri Nouwen entitled *Wounded Healer*, writes that "Nouwen's difficulties with his own father had prevented him from making the father in the [Prodigal Son] painting the center of his attention ... he could not keep pointing to his father as an excuse for his life" (p. 174). In his conferences and books, Henri often struggled with his sense of loneliness. After an inspiring talk on spirituality

173

and solitude to a thousand people or more, Henri would go home alone and lonely. He could share this wound with the whole world through talks and books, but he had great trouble settling down in one place long enough to let himself be known by one person, which is intimacy at its deepest.

Spirituality: The Paradox of Love

As noted throughout this book, couples are called to be simultaneously individuated and connected, autonomous and communal, independent and interdependent. This fundamental contradiction of love, which is a reality in couple relationships, needs to be experienced more than talked about, to be lived more than understood. This "intimacy paradox," as Donald Williamson calls it, is to live a healthy balance between individuation and intimacy in couple relationships, to be intimate and caring while also allowing separation and difference. Murray Bowen asks people to achieve a healthy differentiation within the context of an intimate couple or family relationship. In this paradox, two seemingly contradictory experiences are said to be true at the same time, and as such, form a balanced whole. Indeed, mature people are capable of holding these two truths and lived experiences together. This process of being together separately demands a profound maturity and a deep sense of Being-in-relationship, a sacred place that is well grounded in love. The more mature the differentiation of both partners, the more room for growth in each partner's sense of self and sense of connectedness. Each couple reaches a comfortable balance between individuation and togetherness and finds a balance in this paradox of intimacy. That movement or development of balance often follows a path from "I" to "We" and from "We are" to "We are in relationship."

VanKatwyk writes that "If a relationship is a place of lodgment and germination, it becomes a sacred place where both the self and the relationship can grow" (p. 13). This balancing of self and other in the couple relationship demands trustworthiness and, when wounds overtake us, forgiveness. Being together separately within a couple relationship can be enhanced by a solid spirituality of Being-in-relationship. The command is to love one another as we love ourselves. This means being big enough to see the whole picture of who we are as a couple and as individuals. In this light, the paradox is an invitation to growth.

In his masterpiece book, *The Prophet*, Kahlil Gibran speaks of marriage in this paradoxical manner:

> You were born together, and together you shall be forevermore.
> But let there be spaces in your togetherness.
> And let the winds of the heavens dance between you.
> Love one another, but make not a bond of love:
> Sing and dance together and be joyous, but let each one of you be alone,
> Even as the strings of a lute are alone
> though they quiver with the same music.
> And stand together but not too near together:
> For the pillars of the temple stand apart,
> And the oak tree and the cypress grow not in each other's shadow. (pp. 15–16)

Spirituality: Commitment

Being-in-relationship with each other can also provide the basis for commitment in a couple relationship. Commitment is at the core of intimacy. We know that God is ever faithful, and loves us throughout all of life. God is ever true to the promises (S)He makes. As such, Being-in-relationship with God and being-in-relationship with each other provides the foundation for couple commitment. Couple relationships are about making and keeping promises, and being in relationship can furnish the love and strength needed to commit ourselves to another person and maintain our commitment to the relationship. In a sense, we are naturally driven towards love and relationship – perhaps, at times, in the blindness of being in love – but this drive is real and human nonetheless. In the days of being in love, wild horses could not separate us, but in the days of the dance of wounds, hurts and fears can fog our commitments. Being-in-relationship can be a source of that hope we need to work on the relationship, and forgiveness can be the tool that helps re-create our being in relationship. As Peck says, couple relationships are a lot of work, especially when we are tempted to abandon them. Out beyond whether we are right or our partner is right is a place called commitment; let us meet there where Being-in-relationship meets us and encourages us a couple.

As a therapist, I often tell seriously conflicted couples that they are in the right relationship at this time, even as troubles and couple wounds abound, and I encourage them to hang in there with me for ten to twelve sessions before making any further decisions. Often, the couple conflict is about the dance of wounds, where old family-of-origin patterns have come to visit both partners. These wounds are well worth working out between them; often, when partners can begin to see the origin of their own wounds and the couple dance in the present time, they can begin to make changes in themselves and, therefore, within the couple relationship. A new way of being in relationship is possible. On the other hand, I also tell them that if they run away from this relationship now (unless, of course, it is violent or abusive), they will simply bring the wounds along with them to the next relationship. If they learn only to blame their partner for their present ills, it will be just a matter of time before their old wounds come forward again to ruin another relationship. Dealing with our wounds and committing ourselves to grow now is the best guarantee for happiness in relationship.

Spirituality: Forgiveness

David Augsburger writes that "Since nothing we intend is ever faultless, and nothing we attempt ever without error, and nothing we achieve without some measure of finitude and infallibility we call humanness, we are saved by forgiveness." No couple escapes conflict and frustration within the relationship; partners need to seek and grant forgiveness in order to re-establish peace at various points along their journey. In fact, intimate relationships — with our family of origin, partners or children — can be a constant source of conflict. Often the dance of wounds outlined in Chapter 5 leads to couple offences and therefore requires forgiveness and reconciliation. Sometimes we need to forgive ourselves. The hardest offences to forgive are those that touch our own family-of-origin wounds, for unredeemed wounds are usually covered in strong defensive reactions. Partners need a strong sense of individuation and connectedness to accept their faults and vulnerabilities. In order to forgive and then reconcile, couples must believe in the dignity of their partners, especially the one who hurt them. Only forgiveness can break the dance of wounds. Forgiveness is an indispensable sign of being in relationship.

If Being-in-relationship is the spiritual goal of couples, offences are actions against the relationship and can often do incredible damage to it. A variety of couple offences may need to be forgiven and reconciled: from small, hurtful words to contentious actions. When we trip over an old wound and hurt our partner as a result, an apology and forgiveness are required. When unfulfilled needs creep into the couple relationship and one partner is acting out, forgiveness may be in order. We might need to forgive our parent(s) for the wounds experienced within our family of origin so that we no longer carry the hurt or disappointment we have suffered from them. Siblings often need forgiveness and reconciliation just to move beyond the hurts of sibling rivalry. Perhaps we need to forgive ourselves, to let go of faults and misdeeds from our past.

An affair may be the greatest offence of all. An affair is often a sign of a serious wound seeking fulfillment and soothing. It is a true indication of incongruence or emptiness in the balance between individuation and intimacy – it smashes any sense of trust and innocence in the relationship and forces upon each partner a whole new look at themselves and each other. An affair, which often looks like a thousand lies, is really one big lie lived over time.

Forgiveness is good for the soul, even if our reputation suffers a blow. Forgiveness takes a lot of courage, and loving requires solid confidence in our spirituality. Reaching agreement on a definition of forgiveness has not been easy. Clear differentiation is made between forgiveness and reconciliation, for they are two distinct yet interrelated processes. Forgiveness does not necessarily mean reconciliation; couples need to know the distinction between them. Forgiveness is the work of the offender, who prepares himself or herself to seek and ask for forgiveness. It is also the work of the injured party, who prepares herself or himself to forgive and let go of the offence. Reconciliation, on the other hand, is defined as the restoration of trust in an interpersonal relationship through mutual trustworthy acts of forgiveness. **Forgiveness is seen more as internal and intrapersonal, while reconciliation is interpersonal.** Forgiveness is granted while reconciliation needs to be achieved. Forgiveness is often followed by reconciliation, but not always. For example, one person may be willing to forgive another, but the other refuses to acknowledge fault and therefore reconciliation is not possible. Or the injured party may choose to forgive but not restore full relationship due to the breach of trust. One person can proceed with forgiveness without renewing their engagement with the other. For example, we can forgive our deceased parents for old family-of-origin offences, or forgive someone who hurt us long ago. Forgiveness and reconciliation are part of a cumulative process that takes time – even years. As such, forgiveness (an internal process) sets the stage for reconciliation (an interpersonal reconnecting process) and a re-creation of the couple relationship. Although highly interrelated, we will look at them separately and interrelatedly.

One process of forgiveness/reconciliation for most major couple offences sets out steps built upon the Journey to Maturity, outlined in Chapter I. This model outlines a seven-step process that moves from forgiveness to reconciliation, from independent action to interdependent action, from individuation to connectedness. These steps are depicted as

1. impact,
2. know thyself again,
3. decision to forgive,
4. opening the couple dialogue,
5. conversations of forgiveness and reconciliation,
6. discovering new meaning in old wounds, and
7. a new future.

Forgiveness and Reconciliation in Couple Relationship

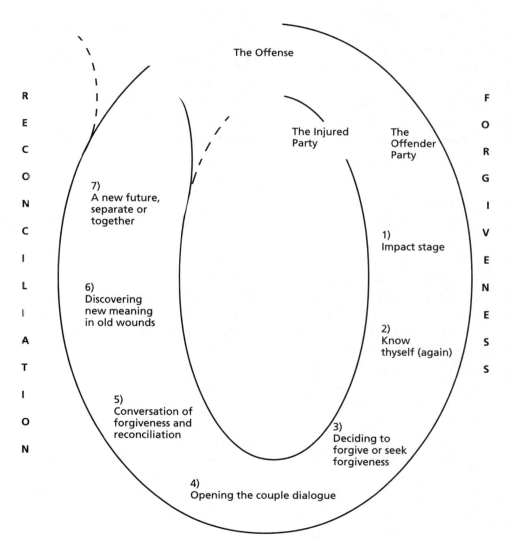

The Offense

The Injured Party

The Offender Party

R
E
C
O
N
C
I
L
I
A
T
I
O
N

F
O
R
G
I
V
E
N
E
S
S

7) A new future, separate or together

6) Discovering new meaning in old wounds

5) Conversation of forgiveness and reconciliation

4) Opening the couple dialogue

3) Deciding to forgive or seek forgiveness

2) Know thyself (again)

1) Impact stage

Step 1 (impact) is the beginning of the journey to forgiveness and reconciliation. The major impact of any offence is that smack in the face, that hurt that comes when someone you love and trust does or says something that offends. Sometimes there is shock and even denial. Forgiveness begins when both partners start to grapple with the offensive experience and the feelings involved. Often partners ask why, wondering and questioning how the offense happened. Both partners – the offender party and the injured party – need to acknowledge, absorb and feel the impact of the offence. Forgiveness begins mainly as an internal process that happens within both parties; each has certain dynamics to deal with, probably in different ways.

Dynamics	Offender Partner	Injured Partner
Feelings	confusion, denial, shame, guilt	hurt, betrayal, anger, shock/denial
Experience	examine the offence	aware of pain: share it with others
Thoughts	how could I do this?	how could (s)he do this?
Behaviours	hiding, running, numbing	crying, grieving, confusion

Step 2 (know thyself again) involves starting to think about yourself in a brand-new way. This step is about seeking understanding and knowing yourself all over again. For the offender, the process of forgiveness is more about humbly accepting responsibility for their actions, with a willingness to make amends; for the injured party, it is more about letting go of hurt and pain. Forgiveness and reconciliation is a slow, thorough and spacious process with many stops along the way as both partners engage in an ongoing individuation process of who they now see themselves to be and how they now want to be connected with the other. Awareness is at the heart of forgiveness: awareness of ourselves and of the other, along with a desire to be liberated from fears, problems and wounds. To move towards forgiveness is to believe one can learn and change.

This is the stage of recognizing the pain both partners feel and the need to work through these feelings to some new thoughtful self-understanding. Each partner needs to deal with their own emotional universe before proceeding to dialogue with each other. We each have a wound or two, and a serious offence probably brings these wounds and accompanying feelings to the fore. Each partner must engage in the work of recognizing their woundedness and how it might have played a part in the offence. Some offences take us back to some distant wound of our family of origin; these are difficult to recognize as we probably have built in strong defensive reactions. This could be the case of the husband who recoils at his wife's finger-pointing because it reminds him so much of his mother's scolding, or the wife who cowers at her husband's tone because of instant reminders of her father's anger. On the other hand, partners need to be aware of possible resistance in moving toward forgiveness. Sometimes we are just not ready to deal with certain offences because old wounds have not yet been addressed or healed. Only when we have identified and healed our own wounds will we be able to forgive others for theirs. We may need to learn to accept certain things in ourselves and in each other, as well as things that need to be changed before partners can individually move towards forgiveness and reconciliation.

Dynamics	Offender Partner	Injured Partner
Feelings	confused, depressed, troubled	angry, maybe hating; vulnerable
Experience	take responsibility for the offence	I deserve better
Thoughts	facing the music	regroup
Behaviours	to know myself again and forgive myself	to identify my loss

Step 3 (decision to forgive) moves both partners onto the decision whether to seek forgiveness and to forgive. Finding a safe place to make this decision is vital. As suggested in Chapter 8, a secure place can involve being connected with family, supportive people and, for some, God. Turning to God and feeling aware of Being-in-relationship with God might allow partners to find new meaning in the offence and discover reasons to continue the road to forgiveness and reconciliation. This is the stage where partners need to stay solidly in touch with their feelings amidst the internal bargaining that might happen before partners decide if they want to move on to the reconciliation stage. The responsibility for engaging in the forgiveness/reconciliation process lies with both the offender partner and the injured partner.

It is during this stage that the injured partner decides not to seek revenge and the offender partner puts an end to any offending action. Both actions are essential. As long as the offender continues their behaviour, it is impossible to move on to forgiveness. It may take courage for the injured partner to demand that the offender partner cease all offensive actions, even at the risk of ending the relationship. Injured partners have been known to give in too easily or quickly for fear of losing the relationship. Some offenders really don't want to change their behaviour or they stubbornly remain unrepentant. Sometimes, it is necessary just to walk away from the relationship. The injured partner is entitled to their hurt feelings, but focusing on revenge means continuing to live in the past and prevents healing, even if they decide not to renew the relationship. It is important to note here that, on many occasions, the injured partner can forgive the offence, let go of the need for retribution, and release bound up feelings, and yet also decide that the relationship is too gravely damaged to proceed to reconciliation and reconnection.

Forgiveness is not something we can easily will to happen. It usually happens over time; we should be cautious about premature or pseudo-forgiveness, which just makes one person feel better and denies couple differences. Forgiving too soon might be a sign of denial or enmeshment. Both partners need sufficient time to individuate, get their own space and stand on their own feet again. On the other hand, as long as the injured partner holds onto retaliation or remains mired in deep hurt or hate, the next step cannot happen. Waiting too long to forgive might lead to a poisoning resentment and indicates an inability to reconnect and to become intimate again, a sign that the relationship might need to end. Partners need to be careful not to encourage forgiveness before both people have truly taken responsibility for their own behaviour and have done all they can to make restitution for the offence. Partners need to make room for ongoing feelings, including anger and guilt.

Dynamics	Offender Partner	Injured Partner
Feelings	confused, yet determined	hurting, yet willing to see
Experience	I am alone in this	I need the support of others
Thoughts	can I ever be forgiven?	dare I trust him/her again?
Behaviours	decide to seek forgiveness	move towards granting forgiveness

Step 4 (opening the couple dialogue) is the beginning of reconciliation. Reconciliation begins when a couple decides to begin a dialogue about the offense and what each would like to do next. Both partners will, at some point, have to share the impact of the offense upon them, including their feelings (pain, hurt, anger, guilt, hate, shame, etc.). Partners may want to talk about how they now see themselves as a result of the offense, how it has changed them and what they know about themselves now. When both partners come to the point of deciding to move in the direction of forgiving and seeking forgiveness, the offending party must provide corrective experiences that rebuild trust and intimacy.

The injured partner, if willing, tells the other that he or she wants to work on the marriage and do whatever is appropriate to rebuild trust and emotional connectedness. In the case of an affair, it is appropriate to insist upon a reasonable degree of accountability for such things as time away from home, phone calls, monetary expenses and any other related conditions in order to continue to live together. Demand that the offender partner end all contact with his or her lover. The offender partner might need to be asked to leave the house for a while, if the injured partner's requests are not being met. It is mostly left to the injured party to determine if and when overtures of forgiveness might be responded to and if forgiveness will be given.

One of the main pieces of conversation is creating a safe enough space for both partners to talk about feelings as a result of the offense. The injured partner needs to be able to talk about the hurt, betrayal, disintegration of trust, confusion and anger. Anger is especially difficult to express and to hear, but healing can only happen through conversation and connection. For the offender partner, feelings of shame, confusion and especially guilt need to come out.

Vulnerability is the spiritual exercise of letting go of old relationship patterns and arguments, and daring to create new meaning and purpose in the present realities of the offense. The offender may still be in love with the person with whom they had the affair, while wanting to try to reconcile with their partner. One partner's being in love with two people at the same time can muddy the relationship, the conversation and the feeling for a while. Such an offender partner needs time to grieve the loss of love with the other person while beginning to rediscover a new love for their partner. All this will take time — indeed, months — during which both partners are holding and expressing a variety of confused and mixed feelings. As suggested in Chapter 6 (Communication), this might be a good time for the 10/10 dialogue or the eagle feather, two methods that give each partner time and space to express themselves without fear of interruption or emotional interference.

Dynamics	Offender Partner	Injured Partner
Feelings	guilty and hopeful, pleading	scared, cautious, vigilant
Experience	to be open and honest	let's see what (s)he says and does
Thoughts	trying to understand myself	open to understand the offender
Behaviours	cautiously talking; forgiving self admission of wrongdoing	cautiously listening; letting go

Step 5 (conversations of forgiveness and reconciliation) has both partners engage in various conversations. Forgiveness/reconciliation means allowing the offender to rebuild trust in the relationship through acting in a trustworthy manner as well as promoting an open discussion of the relational violation, so that the injured party and the offender can agree to work towards an improved reconciliation and healing. Understanding and insight in this dialogue also need to focus on what happened before the offense and how both parties might have contributed to the conflictual situation.

These conversations of forgiveness and reconciliation require 1) taking a stance of individuation (talk nicely; honesty), 2) becoming more connected and appreciative of the other (listen well; empathy), and 3) facing wounds still dancing in the couple relationship (don't be scared). Forgiveness/reconciliation begins with truth-telling. It involves, first of all, an entry into oneself, into one's feelings and solitude and a search for who each person is now. It also involves confronting the offender partner, and putting on the table what they know and feel about the offense. Forgiveness demands, above all, a lot of conversation and getting to know oneself and the other all over again. In part, this is the spiritual process of knowing and being known in real-life action. It necessitates mutual sharing: both partners must talk honestly about the offense and identify their feelings.

In part, this stage demands that the injured partner try to understand the offender and see his or her actions in the broader light of her or his own woundedness. Understanding the offender here does not mean excusing them or letting them get away without blame; it means thoughtfully trying to bring human compassion and empathy into an emotionally laden situation. As partners engage in the conversation, they must keep eyes and ears wide open to learn aspects of their partner that they may not have known before. These conversations are not meant to be a blame game, but a way to see the "why" behind the other partner, help each other unpack old wounds, and maybe even find new, positive, unknown aspects in each other. While the couple was "in love" they saw certain expressions of each other; after an offense, a whole new set of personality dynamics becomes exposed. Both the good and the bad, the "better" and the "worse" are in fact real chapters of both partners' lives.

Dynamics	Offender Partner	Injured Partner
Feelings	bashful, ashamed, hopeful	cautious, open, sanguine
Experience	I'm scared to talk about this	open to possibility of reconciliation
Thoughts	stop trying to get it over with	stop trying so hard to forgive
Behaviours	telling the story over and over demonstrate behaviour is changed	listening for truth and gaps

Step 6 (discovering new meaning in old wounds) seeks a new set of relationship beliefs and values as a result of the offense and the new place in which the couple finds themselves. Partners are trying to make sense of life again. Ultimately, each partner needs to be able to find and give some meaning to the experience. As such, forgiveness is primarily a spiritual exercise that seeks to bring wholeness back into the relationship and give the couple a renewed sense of meaning and purpose. Sometimes, Being-in-relationship can turn bad things to good for those who seek. One aspect of reconciliation is a change in motivation towards the offender partner, in the sense of reaching for the one who offended. It is a voluntary sharing that must be repeated gently, day after day after day. In this sense, reconciliation is that "religion/*religare*" activity of bringing together or reconnecting – knowing and being known all over again. This process involves reviewing family-of-origin wounds and wondering how these may have been operative in this offense. Each person needs the ability and willingness to see their part in the conflict and make amends in areas they need to change. Overt acts of forgiveness are essentially the work of the offending party to rebuild trust by acts and words, which, over time, create a new trusting story between the partners. Forgiveness therefore means entering into vulnerability and seeking a deeper spiritual awakening within oneself and one's partner.

At some point, the conversation must move to the next step, which includes what each partner knows about the other, and how they see each other after the offense. Building a safe and secure bond by rebuilding trust is possible only through intensive listening and developing a new appreciation about the other. This stage helps couples grapple with meaning-making after the offense, and begin to create insight and perspective in the dynamics of their whole lives. A new connectedness needs to be established, and the torn-up road of trust rebuilt.

Forgiveness/reconciliation cannot happen unless each partner wants to and tries to understand the other, and appreciates what might have led up to the offense. Understanding and appreciation do not mean acceptance, but they can open the way to further communication and knowing.

During this stage of forgiveness/reconciliation, partners need to focus on and be sensitive to each other's family-of-origin wounds, for these have usually been dancing in the couple relationship that led up to the offense in the first place. It is especially important here to move from hurt and anger to understanding of how one partner could have offended, or how they as a couple originally got to this situation of couple distance. Where were they, as a couple, before the offense happened? What wound or need was left unmet that caused one partner to damage the relationship? At some stage, these conversations will mean that both partners let go of the hurt and anger and guilt and move to a place of forgiveness/reconciliation.

Lastly, and probably most important, the conversation must turn fearlessly to possible underlying problems and individual wounds that are part of the couple relationship as well as of each individual, probably prior to the offense. This involves entering into and talking about each one's own problems, wounds, struggles, sins and the darker corners of personality that they would prefer to leave undisturbed. When a couple can begin to face the pain and issues together, deeper change and relationship can result. Even if divorce is the eventual outcome, both partners will have a better knowledge of themselves for the future. This is the honest owning up, the expansion of meaning, the insight into self that opens the way for deep healing and real marriage dialogue. Offering a heartfelt apology is vital here. The real changes that the offender partner begins to live help guarantee a successful reconciliation. In whatever way possible, the couple needs to learn to "walk down another street" of living their relationship, emotionally and spiritually.

Forgiving, being forgiven and becoming reconciled is an involved process that requires a deep understanding of ourselves and our partner. When we see our partner as someone who, at times, does wrong, just as we do wrong; when we see that our partner has wounds and can hurt us out of those wounds, just as we have our wounds; when we see that our partner does not necessarily intend to be mean, just like we make mistakes, then we can learn to appreciate our partner as a human being, just like us, neither better nor worse. Compassion and empathy are the ability to see our partner and other people as being a whole lot like us, to hold our partner with all their gifts and wounds. To reconnect with our partner after going through a serious offense is like beginning again the process of getting to know each other and working on re-creating the couple relationship in a whole new way. This may not solve all your problems, but it is an excellent beginning. Working through the seven steps of forgiveness and reconciliation is one couple activity that will need to be repeated, as Jesus says, "seven times seventy" times in the life of the relationship.

Dynamics	Offender Partner	Injured Partner
Feelings	cleansing, relief	relief, accepted
Experience	I am okay	I am okay
Thoughts	I have another chance to love	I have learned a lot
Behaviours	express regret, change behaviour	express forgiveness
	articulate lessons learned	seek deeper meaning

Step 7 (the future) is really the final decision time. Here, one or both partners decide to try a new future together or to break up. Partners need to engage in conversations with each other about who they now see themselves to be, and what future each wants to make together, both immediately and in the longer term. This could mean that the relationship is heading towards termination, is put on hold or is in renewal. As we said earlier, here is where we differentiate forgiveness from reconciliation, for it may be that after all this internal work and after all these conversations, one or both partners may come to the conclusion that the couple relationship needs to end. Even if all this work does not lead to reconciliation, it is nevertheless beneficial to those who forgive and an important learning activity for both partners on their own journey in love and relationships.

Forgiveness and reconciliation take time – sometimes a lot of time. It is wise that couples not rush into reactive decisions after a serious offense, but rather engage in the journey of reflecting upon themselves as individuals, as a couple and as a family. Forgiveness is an arduous process of re-establishing trust. It is crucial to assess readiness for reconciling. Forgiveness does not mean forgetting, and when memories come back, perhaps activated by anniversaries or encounters, feelings will return. Couples need room to talk about them openly. Indeed, after a serious offense, the old couple relationship is forever changed. It will be impossible to go back to the way it was for the simple reason that the old relationship no longer exists, and cannot be refound.

Dynamics	Offender Partner	Injured Partner
Feelings	relieved, hopeful	cautious, hopeful
Experience	learning from my mistakes	learning from my mistakes
Thoughts	I need to make changes in me	I need to stay true to myself
Behaviours	open, generous, connecting	open, letting go, connecting

Family systems theory, especially family of origin and couple relationships, is particularly appropriate for forgiveness/reconciliation interventions. Forgiveness/reconciliation is a central ingredient in balancing independence and interdependence in couple and family relationships. The process of forgiveness/reconciliation may be linear or cyclical, sequential or simultaneous, yet healing often begins in the first step, when both partners are willing to start talking about what they now know about themselves, especially their feelings of hurt, guilt, anger, disappointment, betrayal, being lost. Seen through the eyes of family-of-origin therapy, forgiveness/reconciliation is a multigenerational healing process. Forgiveness involves becoming aware of and healing past wounds, acknowledging present feelings and stating future wants. Forgiveness can encompass a renewed relationship with a partner, but it also demands a review of relationships with parents and other significant family members. It catapults both parties into an ongoing process of deepening individuation, of re-establishing intimacy and connection and of facing intimidations that may have lay dormant for years. Both partners need to be able to understand the origins of their partner's past wounds and how this might have been activated through an offense. Couples can be guided into and through their problems or wounds by means of a detailed family map.

Forgiveness/reconciliation is one of the high roads to inner peace and deeper spirituality. If couple offenses touch the partners' wounds, the process of forgiveness can, in fact, be a gift, a lesson that forces them to examine their wounds and move in the direction of healing and growth. Forgiveness is letting go of the past, letting go of any misperceptions or hurts. It is in this process of forgiving and letting go that we are open to embrace the present and live in the now, for the now is the only place where real love and God dwell.

Example: Marian's Story

Marian had been sexually abused as a child by her father. At the age of 54, she was bringing these stories to therapy and slowly divulging the experience and her present feelings. She began to write poetry and to illustrate some of her experiences, first in pencil, and later in paintings. Her paintings gradually began to reveal a constant and unfailing light somewhere in the background of her paintings, sometimes bright, other times faded, but always present. In time, she was able to put the word "God" to that light, which gradually developed into a felt sense of "Presence" in some of her experiences. Little by little she could acknowledge that she was not alone, even in her times of being abused. Bit by bit she told stories of her father's mental afflictions, his severe childhood wounds, and the terrible state of her parents' marriage. She began to see her father as more than just an abuser, and as she did this, Marian could slowly forgive him.

Conclusion

Research has also shown that "families who pray together, stay together" more often, with lower divorce rates. Marriages are enhanced when there is room for spiritual values in the relationship and in the couple conversations. Spiritual sharing is often the most intimate conversation couples can have. It offers a deeper meaning to life's experiences and emotions, from wonder and awe to pain, suffering and death. Spirituality can be a powerful resource during times of stress and life transitions, giving meaning, stability, purpose to life and forgiveness/reconciliation.

The Smaller Beatitudes for Couples

Blessed are those who can laugh at themselves:

they will have no end of fun.

Blessed are those who can tell a mountain from a molehill:

they will be saved a lot of bother.

Blessed are those who know how to relax without looking for excuses:

they are on their way to becoming wise.

Blessed are those who know when to be quiet and listen:

they will learn a lot of new things.

Blessed are those who are sane enough not to take themselves seriously:

they will be valued by those about them.

Happy are you if you take small things seriously and face serious things calmly:

you will go far in life.

Happy are you if you can appreciate a smile and forget a frown:

you will walk on the sunny side of the street.

Happy are you if you can be kind in understanding the attitudes of others:

you will achieve clarity.

Blessed are those who think before they act and pray before they think:

they will avoid many blunders.

Happy are you if you know how to hold your tongue and smile:

peace has begun to seep into your soul.

—*Author Unknown*

To "Let Go" Takes Love

To - LET GO - does not mean to stop caring. It means I can't do it for someone else.

To - LET GO - is not to cut myself off. It is the realization that I can't control another.

To - LET GO - is not to try to change or blame another, it is to make the most of myself.

To - LET GO - is not to judge but to allow another to be a human being.

To - LET GO - is not to be protective, it is to allow another to face reality.

To - LET GO - is not to deny but to accept.

To - LET GO - is not to adjust each day to my desires, but to take each day as it comes.

To - LET GO - is not to forget the past, but to grow and live for the future.

To - LET GO - is to fear less and to love more.

—*Author Unknown*

Exercise I: Spirituality

The purpose of this exercise is to share aspects of your spirituality with your partner so that you might know each other better and connect with and support each other on your spiritual journey.

Some important aspects of my spirituality are

1)

2)

3)

Some important aspects I notice in your spirituality are

1)

2)

3)

Exercise 2: Forgiveness

This is a truth-telling exercise that might be good to do once a year, a sort of confession of hurts and a desire to connect more intimately. It is also an exercise that puts on the table of couple discussion what is usually known under the surface.

Things I need to let go of and forgive are

1)

2)

3)

Things I need to accept in our relationship are

1)

2)

3)

Things I want to change in our relationship are

1)

2)

3)

Conclusion:
A Family-of-Origin Story

It had been 13 years since we all were in one room; 13 years since I had left home to go work in a faraway place, hoping that the geographical cure might soothe the deep pain in my gut; 13 years since Mom and Dad and my big brother, Joe, and I sat around one table. Thirteen years and it all felt like yesterday. Everyone was over at our house for Christmas dinner this Sunday between Christmas and New Year's. We even knew our old places around the table: Dad in the chair in the corner, Mom closest to the kitchen, and Joe and I in the back, with Joe sitting closer to Mom and me closer to Dad. That is the way it usually was. My husband kept busy serving and cleaning up. I had even cooked our favourite family dish, remembered from my childhood. It was Christmas and how good to be together again, I thought, here, together in my house now.

I had so looked forward to this day. Memories filled the air and the laughter of our family life around dinner tables such as this one rang in my ears. There had been so many occasions to celebrate in those days, and Mom was a great cook. So I remembered. But then, even as I remembered all that, I was also beginning to feel a recurring heartache that was also part of my childhood memories.

I left home when I was 18 years old, in part to seek a better education elsewhere. They say that, in those days, the only way out of Nova Scotia was to go to university elsewhere in the country or to become a priest! Maybe I just needed to get out of the house. My parents and I did not always see eye to eye.

Joe left home two years before I did. It had taken him a while to finish his education, but in the end, he succeeded in his dream of becoming an engineer. And yet, he never seemed to have any money or any time to come home for a visit. I had been home several times, but Joe was never able to make it. He always had some good excuse that Mom and Dad accepted; he was always busy with life. They always said that he would come home if he could. They also never asked any deeper questions.

Dad looked older now, but then again, it had been 13 years, and all these years have not been so kind to his health. Dad had retired and was constantly fixing the house. Mom was quiet, which was her usual self when there were too many others around, especially men. She seemed to give way to them, even if I knew she did this resentfully. At times I would hear about the fights Mom and Dad got into, a sort of old dance in which each one instinctively knew the steps of how to hurt the other. It had been rehearsed for years. Sooner or later, they got over whatever the quarrel was about and went on. It took me some years to get it into my head that it was their dance now, and I did not have to intervene, feel sorry for either of them or try to fix it.

But all that is history and this was Christmas dinner with my family.

"Son," said Dad, not long into the supper, "you have done so well for yourself. I am proud of you. I am always amazed at how you learn all those things by yourself. You are the genius of the family."

It hit me like an arrow in the heart, but felt like an old familiar pain in the gut. Then hurt changed to anger. How dare he say that! I was the one who paid their airfare so they could come here and we could all meet together for the first time in 13 years! I had arranged this! It was my home and my meal they were eating! In fact, it was I who usually reached out to Mom and Dad over the years, by phone and mail. My genius brother hardly did any of that, except when I reminded him to. The fact is I took care of him often enough as well. That role in the family had fallen onto me, that sense of over-responsibility and duty.

Still, Dad's words slammed like an old pain, yet a pain so familiar, a mantra I had heard a hundred times before, when I was younger. Joe was always Mom's favourite child, and in later years Dad preferred "man-to-man" conversations with his son. He never did have much appreciation for the abilities of women, including his wife, and, in case I might have forgotten since I left home, me. In fact, that is why I had left home, as I stopped to think about it. A familiar wound, from old times, for all times. Damn it!

I got up from the table, hoping that no one noticed my pained face. I went to the sink. My husband was right behind me, having excused himself to get some more wine. He came behind me and whispered in my ear "Sermon Number 2," rubbed my shoulder and went back to the table. I knew Sermon Number 2 by heart.

Sermon Number 1, Dad's favourite and most-used conversation line, could be summed up as follows: "Things go wrong because people do not pray enough." I had worked through the memory and feelings of that sermon pretty well, and was quite able to scoff it off as a measure of Dad's old-time Catholic faith. Even Sermon Number 3 no longer wore on me like before. Sermon Number 3, which was more Mom's sermon, simply stated, "People who have pre-marital sex go to hell." It took me a while to name and claim the effect that sermon had on me, especially in my teenage years, but now, I could pass that sermon over to old Father Murphy, our long-time parish priest, who would use that line in his sermons more often than I even thought of sex. Perhaps he was the one with an issue about sex!

But I was still working through Sermon Number 2 in therapy. Its basic line, its tone and insinuation, was that my older brother was the favourite child, and I was second fiddle, no matter how hard I tried to please Dad and Mom. From day one, he was the firstborn, the favourite, the one who could do no wrong, Mr. Untouchable! And for one time in their married lives, Mom and Dad were pretty much on the same page with that sermon. To hear it again, this Christmas season, at this gathering that I had arranged, just hurt.

I collected my thoughts standing at the sink, and remembered the thoughtful and measured response that I had been practising for months as preparation for this family gathering. The therapist had warned me that I could expect all of the old sermons, tones and feelings to come back as a flood during the family reunion. I took a big breath and returned to the table.

"Dad," I said, trying to break a bit of a smile, "isn't it great that Joe has done so well. By the way, I haven't told you yet, but I was just offered a new teaching job, the one I always wanted to do. It is a dream come true. I remember as a child that I always wanted to be a teacher, and now that is real."

Mom and Joe turned to me with smiles and congratulations. Dad picked up his wineglass and proposed a toast. "So, I see that we have two geniuses in the family! Congratulations, my daughter!"

When my husband turned his glass of wine to me for the toast, he winked. It felt like my gut and my heart were beginning to heal.

Autobiography in Five Short Chapters

by Portia Nelson

Chapter One

I walk down the street.
> There is a deep hole in the sidewalk.
> I fall in.
> I am lost ... I am helpless.
>> It isn't my fault.
It takes forever to find a way out.

Chapter Two

I walk down the same street.
> There is a deep hole in the sidewalk.
> I pretend I don't see it.
> I fall in again.
I can't believe I am in the same place.
>> But, it isn't my fault.
> It still takes a long time to get out.

Chapter Three

I walk down the same street.
> There is a deep hole in the sidewalk.
> I see it there.
> I still fall in ... It's a habit ... but
>> My eyes are open.
>> I know where I am.
It is my fault.
I get out immediately.

Chapter Four

I walk down the same street.
There is a deep hole in the sidewalk.
I walk around it.

Chapter Five

I walk down another street.

Glossary

Attachment rests on a process that seeks to regulate our proximity-seeking and contact-maintaining attachment behaviours with one or a few specific individuals who provide us with physical or psychological safety and security. At first this attachment is with our parents; then it moves to our partners and children. Attachment behaviour is an innate motivating activity that promotes closeness/connection or fear/avoidance to one's attachment figure. To feel secure and safe is the primary purpose for attachment behavior.

The **avoidant partner** is uncomfortable getting too close to others even though they do want love relationships. Such partners may be less trusting of others because of childhood hurts. They worry about getting hurt. This worry tends to hold back aspects of love with their partner and they suppress attachment needs or avoid distressing attachment engagement. Such a partner would communicate clearly that they prefer to have plenty of space and distance in the relationship, if they enter into a relationship at all.

Communication: Three simple rules make up the core theory of good communication in couple relationships so that love can grow and partners can thrive: 1) talk nice; 2) listen well; and 3) don't be scared.

Couple spirituality is about Being-in-relationship, whether that is being-in-relationship with our partner, family, children, others or nature, or Being-in-relationship with God and God with each of us.

Differentiation or maturity is that balancing of individuation and intimacy. It permits a mature person to function individually and yet be emotionally involved with others, and to do both simultaneously at a profound depth.

Emotional connectedness is the ability to balance individuation and intimacy/togetherness in such a way that we can both live and love with a good understanding and appreciation of who we are, and do this loving in a space that is secure and safe for both partners.

Emotional cut-off describes the way people manage their undifferentiation by immature separation or distancing from important relationships, especially parents and partners. Cut-off can be enforced through physical distance and/or various forms of withdrawal.

Enmeshment is defined as ways that people give up their own self in order to please others. Enmeshed people have never resolved or untangled the original symbiotic relationship with mother and/or father, and desperately seek togetherness by being loved, accepted or guided though life.

Family of origin includes parents and siblings and is that place where we learned a set of established interactions, rules, beliefs, stances in communication and ways to resolve differences and conflict. These are learned in childhood and pretty much set in place for the rest of our lives, continuing into adulthood.

Individuation refers to a person's ability to operate in an autonomous manner without being impaired by significant others and without feeling overly responsible for them. The individuated person is oriented by principles and can assume personal responsibility without too much fear or guilt. Briefly described, individuation implies that the individual assumes responsibility for his or her own thoughts, feelings and actions.

Intimacy is described as voluntary connectedness. It speaks of an appreciation of others and a closeness that brings out trust and reassurance. Intimacy denotes interdependence and connectedness and a place of emotional safety. Intimacy is that capacity and willingness to want to love and to know one's partner. It demonstrates signs of appreciation and closeness and involves a deep, continuous and honest engagement and communication with one's partner.

Know thyself means that I need to take responsibility for my own contribution to any problem/issues in the relationship with my partner. Most partners have a tendency to ignore their own starring role in the couple conflict and prefer to focus on their partner's flaws.

The **preoccupied partner** wants more intimacy with their partner – probably too much. This partner tends to suffocate and cling to the other. They feel insecure when the other does not seem to love enough or as much as they expect or demand. They are so preoccupied with their need to have another person there for them that they fear individuating and moving on their own.

The **secure partner** can get close to others and is secure in allowing others to become close to them. This partner is capable both of giving and receiving love. They have learned to balance individuation and intimacy.

Wounds are places and behaviours and feelings and opinions where we react or respond in an assumed, automatic, almost childlike manner according to old ways learned within our family of origin. We cling to the familiar, to old blueprints of what should be, and we exhibit an automatic reaction that dictates our way through life.

Notes

Chapter 1: Family of Origin

Murray Bowen, who is known as the father of family-of-origin theory and therapy, developed his theory around eight interlocking concepts. The four main constructs are differentiation, emotional system, multigenerational transmission and emotional triangle. The other four are nuclear family, family projection process, sibling position and societal regression. Bowen later began to add the ninth construct of spirituality, but he never finished. The best-known concept is differentiation of self. Differentiation has been defined as the lifelong process of striving to keep one's being in balance through the reciprocal external and internal processes of self-definition and self-regulation, or the ability to balance individuation and intimacy in close relationships. Differentiation is more than other similar-sounding ideas, such as individuation, autonomy or independence. In this book, maturity is the word used to describe differentiation. For more on family-of-origin theory see M. Bowen, *Family Therapy in Clinical Practice* and M. Kerr, & M. Bowen, *Family Evaluations: An Approach Based on Bowen Theory*. Also see J.L. Framo, *Family of Origin Therapy: An Intergenerational Approach*. An excellent work on implementing family-of-origin theory is D. Williamson, *The Intimacy Paradox: Personal Authority in the Family System*. Williamson used the term "personal authority" to describe maturity and differentiation, giving it a meaning of the authority to author your own life as you see best. Some feminist therapists have taken Bowen's theory and developed a more comprehensive description of differentiation of self to include intimacy and connectedness as a core element (see M. McGoldrick & B. Carter, *Advances in Coaching: Family Therapy with One Person* and P. Titelman, *Clinical Applications of Bowen Family Systems Theory*).

Bowen's Scale of Differentiation is Bowen's effort to say that people are different and that we can all find ourselves somewhere along the continuum of differentiated to undifferentiated. It can be considered a sort of maturity scale. The lowest level of undifferentiation scores at 0 while the highest score of differentiation scores at 100. High-scoring people are marked by a functional level of self and the ability to take "I-positions."

People in the 50 to 75 range have increasingly defined convictions and opinions. People on the lower range of undifferentiation have a basic level, live in a feelings-controlled world and are dominated by a subjective reasoning process. Bowen thought no one could score 100 and that any score over 75 represents a very high-level person.

Attachment theory is the brainchild of John Bowlby, although it was Mary Ainsworth who did most of the research in the field. Bowlby grouped individual attachment behaviour into secure and insecure. From these, three attachment patterns for children have been described: secure, avoidant and ambivalent (M.D.S. Ainsworth, M. Blehar, E. Waters & S. Wall, *Patterns of Attachment: A Psychological Study of the Strange Situation*; the fourth, disorganized, was added later (M. Main & J. Solomon, *Procedures for Identifying Infants as Disorganized/disoriented During the Strange Situation*). Hazen and Shaver used Ainsworth et al.'s attachment patterns as descriptors for adult relationships. Bartholomew and Herowitz followed a similar pattern but broke avoidant into two subgroups, "fearful" and "dismissive."

Chapter 2: My Wounds, As Best I Know Them

Much has been written on the place and role of sibling position in the development of personality and wounds. For more detail, see W. Toman, *Family Constellation: Its Effects on Personality and Social Behavior.* Although research has not been able to establish clear findings regarding the role of sibling position and other personality characteristics, general patterns have been elaborated and can serve as a guide.

Chapter 3: Falling in Love Blinds Us to the Wounds

M. Scott Peck's bestselling *The Road Less Traveled: A New Psychology of Love, Traditional Values and Spiritual Growth,* although an older book, is still read by many and presents a profound and mature way of looking at adult responsibility in life, including love. Peck discusses the process of mature growth, the nature of loving relationships, how to recognize partner compatibility, how to become your own person, and how to distinguish dependency from love. Although much older, Eric Fromm's *The Art of Loving* continues as a classic for all. Also see Leo Buscaglia, *Loving Each Other: The Challenge of Human Relationships,* as well as his other books.

For books on the theory and research of falling in love, see A.M. Pines, *Falling in Love: Why We Choose the Lovers We Do* and D.H. Felmlee, *Fatal Attractions: Affections and Disaffections in Intimate Relationships.*

I have always liked the breakthrough work of Harville Hendrix, *Getting the Love You Want: A Guide for Couples.* In his creation of Imago Therapy, he touches upon the family of origin and inner psychic roots of love and love needs, and encourages partners to move towards the conscious marriage.

Chapter 4: The Honeymoon is Over

Although everyone knows that honeymoons come to an end, there is not much written on why or how this really happens. Many couples express that they thought they had a good relationship going and then wonder how they ever got to this stage of conflict. I have found Lori Heyman Gordon's book *Love Knots* to be truly insightful about all those unmet or unspoken expectations and assumptions that, when left unchecked or not responded to, can sink many relationships by means of a slow, gradual drifting into not caring.

Chapter 5: The Dance of Wounds

Sue Johnson's work on emotionally focused therapy does an expert job of delineating the steps in the dance of wounds. (See S. Johnson, *Creating Connections: The Practice of Emotionally Focused Therapy.*) The development of Emotionally Focused Therapy (EFT) has helped foster the inclusion of emotion and attachment in the area of couple development. EFT is a synthesis of experiential/gestalt and systemic approaches to couples, with up-front inclusion of emotions being a crucial element in couple therapy.

Chapter 6: Know Thyself

Doing a family map or genogram may look complicated at first, but there are several good books to guide couples in this work, and once they begin, many people find they develop a curiosity to know more about themselves and their family of origin. Going home and sitting with parents, listening to their stories of your childhood days are ways to glean the attachment styles that make up your personal history. For more on doing family maps, see M. McGoldrick & R. Gerson, *Genograms in Family Assessment*; R.W. Richardson, *Family Ties that Bind: A Self-help Guide to Change Through Family of Origin Therapy*; and R. Sherman, *The Intimacy Genogram.*

Partners with a **secure/differentiated** attachment pattern tend to describe their family-of-origin experiences with themes such as consistently responsive (Holmes, 1997); sense of personal identity; positive view of self and others (Bartholomew & Horowitz, 1991);

"easy to get close to others" (Hazen & Shaver, 1990); balanced autonomy and connectedness (Bowen, 1978: McGoldrick & Carter, 2001). They value attachment and can realistically talk about it.

Partners with an **enmeshed/preoccupied** attachment pattern tend to describe their family-of-origin experiences as inconsistently responsive (Holmes, 1997); negative view of self, positive view of others (Bartholomew & Horowitz, 1991); parents lacking in love but not rejecting; parents unreliable; a fight for parental attention; confused discussion of relationships; passive and/or angry speech; dependency; "we-ness" (Bowen, 1978); compulsive caregiving (West & Sheldon-Keller, 1994); and "others are reluctant to get as close as I would like" (Hazen & Shaver, 1990). These adults are still caught in old interactional patterns and tend to be clingy partners.

Partners with an **avoidant/cut-off** attachment pattern often describe their family-of-origin experiences with parents as consistently unresponsive (Holmes, 1997); positive view of self, negative view of others (Bartholomew & Horowitz, 1991); compulsive self-sufficiency (West & Sheldon-Keller, 1994); parents were rejecting, distant, withdrawn, away a lot; false claim to normality; independent, invulnerable and deny need for relationships; "emotional distancing" (Bowen, 1978); detached from feelings; consequences of negative behaviour go unchecked; and "uncomfortable being too close to others" (Hazen & Shaver, 1990). These partners downplay the importance of intimacy in their relationships.

Chapter 7: Communication

There is much written about communication theory and communication skills. This chapter is meant to glean only some of the more helpful aspects of the writings. For more information, read L. Heyman Gordon, *Love Knots*; A. Mehrabian, *Silent Messages: Implicit Communication of Emotions and Attitudes*; and M. Mackay, P. Fanning and K. Paleg, *Couple Skills: Making Your Relationship Work*.

Chapter 8: Emotional Connectedness

Emotionally Focused Therapy (EFT) is fast becoming one of the solid and evidence-based approaches for marital therapy. Dr. Sue Johnson, in conjunction with the work of Dr. Les Greenburg, has developed a therapy based upon the principles of gestalt, systemic and attachment theories.

Chapter 9: Spirituality and Forgiveness

Perhaps most couple relationships today are made up of partners of different religions or different scores on any scale of spirituality. It seems that the last area that is explored in knowing your partner, if it is explored at all, is that of spiritual beliefs and practices. Yet significant differences in spirituality can cause much pain in couples, in terms of marriage ceremony, baptism and initiations, and especially situations where partners might turn to spiritual beliefs when pain and suffering need to be addressed. One helpful book is B.J. Brothers, *Spirituality and Couples: Heart and Soul in the Therapy Process.*

Much has been written on affairs and forgiveness, but one of the best is still J.A. Spring, *After the Affair: Healing the Pain and Rebuilding Trust When a Partner Has Been Unfaithful.* This book deals not only with the present feelings of both the offender partner and the injured partner, but also brings both partners back to look at their relationship prior to the affair and to examine what needs to be healed in all these places.

References

Chapter 1: Family of Origin

Ainsworth, M.D.S., Blehar, M., Waters, E., & Wall, S. (1978). *Patterns of Attachment: A Psychological Study of the Strange Situation.* Hillsdale, NJ: Erlbaum.

Ainsworth, M.D.S. & Wittig, B. (1969). Attachment and exploratory behavior of one-year-olds in a strange situation. In B.M. Foss (ed.), *Determinants of Infant Behavior,* 4, 111–136. London: Methuen.

Bartholomew, K. & Horowitz, L.M. (1991). Attachment styles among young adults: A test of the four-category model. *Journal of Personality and Social Psychology,* 61, 226–244.

Bowen, M. (1976). Theory in the practice of psychotherapy. In P.J. Guerin (ed.), *Family Therapy: Theory and Practice.* New York: Gardner Press.

Bowen, M. (1978). *Family Therapy in Clinical Practice.* New York: Jason Aronson.

Bowlby, J. (1969). *Attachment and Loss: Vol. 1, Attachment.* London: Hogarth Press.

Bowlby, J. (1973). *Attachment and Loss: Vol. 2, Separation.* London: Hogarth Press.

Bowlby, J. (1980). *Attachment and Loss: Vol. 3, Loss.* London: Hogarth Press.

Bowlby, J. (1988). *A Secure Base: Clinical Application of Attachment Theory.* London: Routledge.

Dankoski, M.E. (2001). Pulling on the heart strings: An emotionally focused approach to family life cycle transitions. *Journal of Marital and Family Therapy,* 27, 177–187.

Havestraldt, A.J., Anderson, W.T., Piercy, F.P., Cochran, S.W., & Fine, M. (1985). A family of origin scale. *Journal of Marital and Family Therapy,* 11, 287–297.

Hazan, C., & Shavar, P.R. (1987). Romantic love conceptualized as an attachment process. *Journal of Personality and Social Psychology,* 52, 511–524.

Johnson, S.M. & Grenberg, L.S. (1992). Emotionally focused therapy: Restructuring attachments. In S.H. Budman, M.F. Hoyt, & S. Friedman (eds.), *The First Session in Brief Therapy* (pp. 204–224). New York: Guilford Press.

Johnson, S. (1996). *Creating Connections: The Practice of Emotionally Focused Therapy*. Levittown, PA: Brunner/Mazel.

Kerr, M. & Bowen, M. (1988). *Family Evaluations: An Approach Based on Bowen Theory*. New York: W.W. Norton.

Main, M. & Solomon, J. (1990). Procedures for identifying infants as disorganized/disoriented during the Strange Situation. In M.T. Goldberg, D. Cicchetti, & E.M. Cummings (eds.), *Attachment in the Preschool Years: Theory, Research and Intervention*. Chicago: University of Chicago Press.

McGoldrick, M. & Carter, B. (2001). Advances in coaching: Family therapy with one person. *Journal of Marital and Family Therapy*, 27, 281–300.

McGoldrick, M. & Gerson, R. (1985). *Genograms in Family Assessment*. New York: W.W. Norton.

Simpson, J.A. & Rhodes, W.S. (1998). *Attachment Theory and Close Relationships*, New York: Guildford Press.

Sperling, M.B. & Berman, W.H. (1994). *Attachment in Adults: Clinical and Developmental Perspectives*. New York: Guildford Press.

Sroufe, L.A. & Waters, E. (1977). Attachment as an organizational construct. *Child Development*, 48, 1184–1199.

Titelman, P. (1998). *Clinical Applications of Bowen Family Systems Theory*. New York: Haworth Press.

Weinfield, N.S., Sroufe, L.A., Egeland, B., & Carlson, E.A. (1999). The nature of individual differences in infant-caregiver attachment. In J. Cassidy & P.R. Shaver (eds.), *Handbook of Attachment: Theory, Research and Clinical Applications*. New York: The Guilford Press.

Williamson, D. (1991). *The Intimacy Paradox: Personal Authority in the Family System*. New York: Guilford Press.

Chapter 2: My Wounds, As Best I Know Them

Marney, C. (1976). Tape from Princeton Institute of Theology.

Toman, W. (1976). *Family Constellation: Its Effects on Personality and Social Behavior*. New York: Springer.

Chapter 3: Falling in Love Blinds Us to the Wounds

Bowen, M. (1978). *Family Therapy in Clinical Practice*. New York: Jason Aronson.

Buscaglia, L. (1984). *Loving Each Other: The Challenge of Human Relationships*. New York: Fawcett Columbine.

Felmlee, D.H. (1995). Fatal attractions: Affections and disaffections in intimate relationships. *Journal of Social and Personal Relationships*, 12, 295–311.

Freud, S. (1905). *Three Essays on the Theory of Sexuality*. New York: Basic Books.

Fromm, E. (1936). *The Art of Loving*. New York: Bantom Books.

Hazan, C., & Shaver, P. (1987). Romantic love conceptualized as an attachment process. *Journal of Personality and Psychology*, 52, 511–524.

Hendrix, H. (1988). *Getting the Love You Want: A Guide for Couples*. New York: Harperperennial.

Kerr, M. & Bowen, M. (1988). *Family Evaluations: An Approach Based on Bowen Theory*. New York: W.W. Norton.

McGoldrick, M., & Gerson, R. (1985). *Genograms in Family Assessment*. New York: W.W. Norton.

Nowicki, S.Jr., & Menheim, S. (1991). Interpersonal complementarity and time of interaction in female relationships. *Journal of Research in Personality*, 25, 322–333.

Peck, M.S. (1978). *The Road Less Traveled: A New Psychology of Love, Traditional Values and Spiritual Growth*. New York: Touchstone Books.

Pines, A.M. (1999). *Falling in Love: Why We Choose the Lovers We Do*. New York: Routledge.

Scarf, M. (1987). *Intimate Partners: Patterns in Love and Marriage*. New York: Random House.

Shaikh, T. & Suresh, K. (1994). Attitudinal similarity and affiliation needs as determinants of interpersonal attraction. *Journal of Social Psychology*, 134, 257–259.

Watts, A. (1985). Divine madness. In John Welwood (ed.), *Challenge of the Heart*. Boston: Shambhala.

Chapter 4: The Honeymoon Is Over

Buscaglia, L.F. (1984). *Loving Each Other: The Challenge of Human Relationships.* New York: Fawcett Columbine.

de Bernieres, L. (1994). *Captain Corelli's Mandolin.* London: Martin Secker and Warburg.

Gordon, Lori Heyman. (1990). *Love Knots.* New York: Dell.

Chapter 5: The Dance of Wounds

Bowlby, J. (1969). *Attachment and Loss: Vol. 1, Attachment.* London: Hogarth Press.

Diehl, M., Elnick, A.B., Bourbeau, L.S., & LaLouvie-Vief, G. (1998). Adult attachment styles: Their relations to family context and personality. *Journal of Personality and Social Psychology,* 74, 1656–1669.

Johnson, S. (1996). *Creating Connections: The Practice of Emotionally Focused Therapy.* Levittown, PA: Brunner/Mazel.

Main, M. & Hesse, E. (1990). Parents' unresolved traumatic experiences are related to infant disorganized attachment status: Is frightened and/or frightening parental behavior the linking mechanism? In Greenberg, M.T. & Cicchetti, D. (eds.). *Attachment in the Preschool Years: Theory, Research and Intervention.* Chicago: The University of Chicago Press.

Satir, V., Banmen, J., Gerber, J., & Gomori, M. (1991). *The Satir Model: Family Therapy and Beyond.* Palo Alto: Science and Behavior Books.

Simpson, J.A., & Rhodes, W.S. (1998). *Attachment Theory and Close Relationships,* New York: Guildford Press.

Chapter 6: Know Thyself

Adler, R.A. & Rodman, G. (1982). *Understanding Human Communication.* New York: Holt, Rinehart & Winston.

Allport, G.W. (1961). *Patterns of Growth and Personality.* New York: Holt, Rinehart & Winston.

Bartholomew, K. & Horowitz, L.M. (1991). Attachment styles among young adults: a test of the four-category model. *Journal of Personality and Social Psychology,* 61, 226–244.

Bloomfield, H.H. (1983). *Making Peace with Your Parents: The Key to Enriching Your Life and All Your Relationships.* New York: Ballantine Books.

Bowen, M. (1978). *Family Therapy in Clinical Practice.* New York: Jason Aronson.

Buscaglia, L.F. (1984). *Loving Each Other: The Challenge of Human Relationships.* New York: Fawcett Columbine.

Hazan, C. & Shavar, P.R. (1987). Romantic love conceptualized as an attachment process. *Journal of Personality and Social Psychology, 52,* 511–524.

Holmes, J. (1997). Attachment, autonomy, intimacy: Some clinical implications of attachment theory. *British Journal of Medical Psychology, 70,* 231–248.

Kerr, M. & Bowen, M. (1988). *Family Evaluations: An Approach Based on Bowen Theory.* New York: W.W. Norton.

McGoldrick, M. & Carter, B. (2001). Advances in coaching: Family therapy with one person. *Journal of Marital and Family Therapy, 27,* 281–300.

McGoldrick, M. & Gerson, R. (1985). *Genograms in Family Assessment.* New York: W.W. Norton.

Prest, L.A., Benson, M.J., & Protinsky, H.O. (1998). Family of origin and current relationships influences on codependency. *Family Process. 37,* 513–528.

Rankin-Esquer, L.A., Burnett, C.K., Baucom, D.H., & Epstein, N. (1997). Autonomy and relatedness in marital function. *Journal of Marital and Family Therapy, 23,* 175–190.

Richardson, R.W. (1984). *Family Ties that Bind: A Self-help Guide to Change Through Family of Origin Therapy.* Vancouver: Self-Counsel Press.

Sherman, R. (1993). The Intimacy Genogram. *The Family Journal, 1,* 91–93.

Tomson, P. (1985). Genogram in general practice. *Journal of The Royal Society of Medicine Supplement, 78,* 34–39.

West, M.L. & Sheldon-Keller, A.E. (1994). *Patterns of Relating: An Adult Attachment Perspective.* New York: Guilford Press.

Williamson, D. (1991). *The Intimacy Paradox: Personal Authority in the Family System.* New York: Guilford Press.

Chapter 7: Communication

Bowen, M. (1978). *Family Therapy in Clinical Practice.* New York: Jason Aronson.

Gordon, L.H. (1990). *Love Knots.* New York: Dell.

Kerr, M. & Bowen, M. (1988). *Family Evaluation: An Approach Based upon Bowen Theory.* New York: W.W. Norton.

Mehrabian, A. (1981). *Silent Messages: Implicit Communication of Emotions and Attitudes.* Belmont, CA: Wadsworth.

McKay, M., Fanning, P., & Paleg, K. (1994). *Couple Skills: Making Your Relationship Work.* Oakland, CA: New Harbinger Publications.

Powell, J. (1969). *Why Am I Afraid to Tell You Who I Am?* Niles, IL: Argus Communication.

Rogers, C. (1951). *A Way of Being.* Boston: Houghton Mifflin.

Satir, V. (1988). *The New Peoplemaking.* Palo Alto, CA: Science and Behavior Books.

Satir, V., Banmen, J., Gerber, J., & Gomori, M. (1991). *The Satir Model: Family Therapy and Beyond.* Palo Alto, CA: Science and Behavior Books.

Chapter 8: Emotional Connectedness

Fromm, E. (1936). *The Art of Loving.* New York: Bantom Books.

Gottman, J. (1994). *Why Marriages Succeed or Fail ... And How You Can Make Yours Last.* New York: Fireside Books.

Johnson, S. (1996). *Creating Connections: The Practice of Emotionally Focused Therapy.* Levittown, PA: Brunner/Mazel.

Lerner, H.G. (1989). *The Dance of Intimacy: A Woman's Guide to Courageous Acts of Change in Key Relationships.* New York: Harper & Row.

Merton, T. (1966). *Love and Living.* New York: Farrar, Straus & Giroux.

Peck, M.S. (1978). *The Road Less Traveled: A New Psychology of Love, Traditional Values and Spiritual Growth.* New York: Touchstone Books.

Chapter 9: Spirituality and Forgiveness

Anderson, D.A. & Worthen, D. (1997). Exploring the fourth dimension: Spirituality as a resource for the couple therapist. *Journal of Marital and Family Therapy*, 23, 3–12.

Augsburger, D. (1981). *Caring Enough to Not Forgive.* Ventura: Regal Books.

Berensen, D. (1990). A systemic view of spirituality: God and the twelve-step program as resources in family therapy. *Journal of Strategic and Systemic Therapies*, 9, 50–70.

Bowen, M. (1978). *Family Therapy in Clinical Practice.* New York: Jason Aronson.

Brothers, B.J. (1992). *Spirituality and Couples: Heart and Soul in the Therapy Process.* New York: The Haworth Press.

Denys, J.G. (1997). The religiosity variable and personal empowerment in pastoral counselling. *The Journal of Pastoral Care*, 51, 165–176.

Enright, R.D., Freedman, S., & Rique, J. (1998). The psychology of interpersonal forgiveness. In R.D. Enright & J. North (eds.), *Exploring Forgiveness.* Madison, WI: University of Wisconsin Press.

Ford, M. (2002). *Wounded Healer: A Portrait of Henri J. M. Nouwen.* New York: Image Books/ Doubleday.

Gibran, K. (1972). *The Prophet.* New York: Alfred A. Knopf.

Gordon, K.C. & Baucom, D.H. (1999). A multi theoretical intervention for promoting recovery from extramarital affairs. *Clinical Psychology: Science and Practice*, 6, 382–399.

Gordon, K.C., Baucom, D.H., & Snyder, D.K. (2000). The use of forgiveness in marital therapy. In M.E. McCullough, K.I. Pargament, & C.E. Thoresen (eds.), *Forgiveness: Theory, Research and Practice.* New York: Guilford Press.

Hargrave, T.D. (1994). Families and forgiveness: A theoretical and therapeutic framework. *The Family Journal: Counseling and Therapy for Couples and Families*, 2, 339–348.

Hargrave, T.D. & Sells, J.N. (1997). The development of the forgiveness scale. *Journal of Marital and Family Therapy*, 23, 41–62.

McCullough, M.E., Pargament, K.I., & Thoresen, C.E. (2000). *Forgiveness: Theory, Research and Practice.* New York: Guilford Press.

McCullough, M.E., Worthington, E.L., & Rachal, K.C. (1997). Interpersonal forgiveness in close relationships. *Journal of Personality and Social Psychology*, 73, 321–336.

McPherson-Oliver, M.A. (1994). *Conjugal Spirituality: The Primacy of Mutual Love in Christian Tradition*. Kansas City: Sheed & Ward.

Pingleton, J.P. (1989). The role and function of forgiveness in the psychotherapeutic process. *Journal of Psychology and Theology*, 17, 27–35.

Richards, P.S. & Bergen, A.E. (1997). *A Spiritual Strategy for Counseling and Psychotherapy*. Washington, DC: American Psychological Association.

Rovers, M.W., DesRoches, L., Hunter, P., & Taylor, B. (2000). A family of origin workshop: Process and evaluation. *The Family Journal*, 8, 368–375.

Sells, J.N. & Hargrave, T.D. (1998). Forgiveness: A review of the theoretical and empirical literature. *Journal of Family Therapy*, 20, 21–36.

Spring, J.A. (1996). *After the Affair: Healing the Pain and Rebuilding Trust When a Partner Has Been Unfaithful*. New York: Harper Perennial.

VanKatwyk, P.L. (2003). *Spiritual Care and Therapy: Integrative Perspectives*. Waterloo, ON: Wilfrid Laurier University Press.

Vardey, L. (1995). *God in All Worlds: An Anthology of Contemporary Spiritual Writings*. New York: Vintage Books.

Williamson, D.S. (1991). *The Intimacy Paradox: Personal Authority in the Family System*. New York: Guildford Press.